A Preface to Philosophy

A Preface to Philosophy

Mark B. Woodhouse
Georgia State University

Dickenson Publishing Company, Inc.
Encino, California
Belmont, California

ISBN-0-8221-0164-5
Library of Congress Catalog Card Number: 75-8123

Printed in the United States of America
Printing (last digit): 9 8 7 6 5 4 3 2

For Cristina,
in whom I am sustained

Contents

The Dickenson Series in Philosophy

Philosophy, said Aristotle, begins in wonder—wonder at the phenomenon of self-awareness, wonder at the infinitude of time, wonder that there should be anything at all. Wonder in turn gives rise to a kind of natural puzzlement: How can mind and body interact? How is it possible that there can be free will in a world governed by natural laws? How can moral judgments be shown to be true?

Philosophical perplexity about such things is a familiar and unavoidable phenomenon. College students who have experienced it and taken it seriously are, in a way, philosophers already, well before they come in contact with the theories and arguments of specialists. The good philosophy teacher, therefore, will not present his subject as some esoteric discipline unrelated to ordinary interests. Instead he will appeal directly to the concerns that already agitate the student, the same concerns that agitated Socrates and his companions and serious thinkers ever since.

It is impossible to be a good teacher of philosophy, however, without being a genuine philosopher oneself. Authors in the Dickenson Series in Philosophy are no exceptions to this rule. In many cases their textbooks are original studies of problems and systems of philosophy, with their own views boldly expressed and defended with argument. Their books are at once contributions to philosophy itself and models of original thinking to emulate and criticize.

That equally competent philosophers often disagree with one another is a fact to be explored, not concealed. Dickenson anthologies bring together essays by authors of widely differing outlook. This diversity is compounded by juxtaposition, wherever possible, of classical essays with leading contemporary materials. The student who is shopping for a world outlook of his own has a large and representative selection to choose among, and the chronological arrangements, as well as the editor's introduction, can often give him a sense of historical development. Some Dickenson anthologies treat a single group of interconnected problems. Others are broader, dealing with a whole branch of philosophy, or representative problems from various branches of philosophy. In both types of collections, essays with opposed views on precisely the same questions are included to illustrate the argumentative give and take which is the lifeblood of philosophy.

Joel Feinberg
Series Editor

Preface

An introductory course in philosophy poses a number of unique problems for you, the beginning student. Some philosophical issues may seem strangely unrelated to everyday life, and the methods you will use to investigate these issues may often have no direct counterpart in your prior educational experience. The central purpose of *A Preface to Philosophy* is to correct any misconceptions you may have about philosophy and to give you some tools to use in doing philosophical thinking.

In addition, this text is designed to help you develop an overall picture of philosophy that will endure past the final exam and after your precise knowledge of "who said what" has become dim. This picture will enable you to recognize philosophical issues when you come across them, to see their relevance to a variety of nonphilosophical problems and theories, and to approach them rationally. This is the most important kind of knowledge to obtain in a first encounter with philosophy.

Some philosophers suggest that the best means of achieving such knowledge is to begin with a detailed investigation of particular philosophical problems. Of course, *doing* philosophy is absolutely essential for *understanding* what it is all about. But for many students, to start by investigating particular examples of philosophizing leaves many vitally important questions unanswered. For example, by what criteria does one identify a "philosophically interesting" assertion? Doesn't philosophy boil down to a matter of personal opinion? How is philosophy relevant to my life? Such questions demand answers. This text is intended to help construct a framework that, when continually reinforced, exemplified, and refined by discussion of particular issues, will help you understand and analyze the philosophical topics you will encounter both in and out of the classroom.

Chapters I and II, "Recognizing Philosophical Subject Matter" and "Why Philosophize?" give you a theoretical introduction to the study of philosophy and thus should be read at the beginning of the course. Chapter III, "Doing Philosophy," is designed as a continuing practical aid to investigating philosophical problems. Chapter IV, "Is Philosophical Progress Possible?" is intended to reduce your possible initial skepticism about philosophy. And, the final chapter, "Writing Philosophy," presents specific methods that you will use in writing philosophy papers.

This text is not meant as a substitute for becoming critically involved through reading and analyzing primary sources and studying critical commentaries. The various philosophical issues that appear throughout the book are intended to illustrate, generate interest, and prepare you for your first encounter with one of the oldest and most stimulating intellectual disciplines.

Acknowledgments

For their encouragement and helpful suggestions I am indebted to Pat Murray, Neal Buffalo, Kirk Wilson, Grant Luckhardt, Robert Arrington, Robert Almeder, Russell Godwin, to the reviewers, who offered many useful comments and criticisms, and to my students, who suffered through early drafts of the manuscript. For help in collecting exercises and proofreading the manuscript I thank Alfredo Villar and Kathy Weeks. In particular, I wish to thank Howard Pospesel who, from the earliest stages, offered constant encouragement and many detailed criticisms.

I am especially indebted to Professor Steven M. Sanders of the Department of Philosophy, Bridgewater State College, Bridgewater, Massachusetts, who coauthored Chapter V.

My wife, Cristina, made many useful suggestions and provided the moral support essential to my continuing the project.

A Preface to Philosophy

Chapter I

Recognizing Philosophical Subject Matter

The term 'philosophy' encompasses a wide variety of different and not always consistent interpretations. For the early Greeks, 'philosophy' meant literally "love of wisdom." But the responses to the obvious question "What is wisdom?" seldom help to clarify the definition. In contemporary usage, you have probably heard the term employed in many contexts. To have a philosophy might mean to have a point of view, a set of rules for conducting one's life, or some specific values. A person's philosophy, for example, may be that might makes right or that the end justifies the means. Sometimes 'philosophy' is used to connote anything bizarre or even occult, such as astrology or cosmic consciousness. Or the term may be used to suggest that certain beliefs are merely expressions of personal opinion. Moreover, many students tend to associate philosophy exclusively with humanistically oriented studies, not realizing that mathematics and science, too, involve philosophical issues.

Given this diversity of opinion, how shall we undertake to determine the scope of philosophy? One time-honored approach is to present brief definitions of its various subdivisions and then conjoin these with specific examples. This approach is a good way to obtain a general idea of the breadth and complexity of philosophical subject matter. The following are some of the representative subdivisions of philosophy.

1. *Logic:* A study of the principles by which we distinguish sound from unsound reasoning. For example, what is a deductive argument? Why is the argument "All dogs are cats; Socrates is a dog; therefore, Socrates is a cat" valid? (Note: The subject matter of logic is more akin to mathematics than to philosophy. Yet traditionally, philosophers have taught logic, made it an integral part of their investigations, and advanced the discipline to its present state.)

2. *Ethics:* A study of the concepts and principles that underlie our evaluations of human behavior. By what standards ought we distinguish between morally right and wrong actions? Is pleasure the only basis for describing a state of affairs as "good"? Is moral decision arbitrary?

3. *Metaphysics:* A study of the ultimate nature of reality. Can persons exercise freedom of choice? Does a God exist? Is reality essentially spiritual or material? Do persons have minds distinct from their bodies?

4. *Epistemology:* A study of the origin, nature, and extent of knowledge. Is experience the only source of knowledge? What makes some beliefs true and others false? Are there meaningful questions that science cannot answer? Can we know the thoughts and feelings of other persons?

5. *Aesthetics:* A study of the principles implicit in our evaluations of different art forms. What is the purpose of art? What is the role of feeling in aesthetic judgment? How would one determine a great work of art?

This list of classical subdivisions of philosophy can easily be extended to include issues found at the periphery of many standard academic disciplines, such as history, political science, religion, natural and social science, and mathematics. Although citing further philosophical topics related to these disciplines would no doubt increase respect for the breadth and complexity of philosophical subject matter, doing so would leave an important question unanswered: "What do these extremely divergent topics have in common which renders them of *philosophical* interest in the first place?" We need to establish some identifying criteria broad enough to encompass the diversity of philosophical subject matter, yet specific enough to enable us to recognize a particular philosophical issue when we come across it. The purpose of this chapter is to provide these criteria.

Before undertaking the task of defining philosophical subject matter, we must make two preliminary qualifications. First, it is probably impossible to provide a rigid set of characteristics for distinguishing conclusively between what counts as a philosophical problem and what does not. Indeed, the question of what constitutes a philosophical problem is itself a matter of philosophical controversy. But the existence of borderline cases will not prohibit us from surveying the characteristics of a broad range of *core* philosophical topics. Second, none of the criteria we shall consider are individually unique to philosophy. These criteria should therefore be viewed as approximations that, when applied *collectively*, provide a reasonably adequate definition of a philosophical problem.

Philosophical problems are about concepts.

Each of us describes and interprets his experience and the world around him by means of a broad range of concepts, such as 'cause', 'authority', 'truth', 'beauty', 'love', and 'time', expressed in specific claims. For example, we might say: "Every event has a cause"; "Time passes so quickly"; and "Jones fails to exercise his authority." Philosophical problems emerge when we step back from our personal and professional involvements and begin to think critically *about* certain concepts and the beliefs that incorporate them.[1] It is one thing, for example, to label someone as "immoral" in casual conversation at a cocktail party and quite another to explain the distinction between morality and immorality and to justify that distinction with sound arguments.

To say that philosophical problems are about concepts means that they are not about individual things. Rather, philosophical problems are about the concepts used in classifying and describing individual things. For example, what catches the philosopher's eye concerning the statement "Ralph told the truth" is not the potential issue of whether Ralph actually told the truth. Instead, the philosopher's curiosity is aroused by the challenge of determining the standards that *any* sentence in principle must meet in order to merit the label 'truth' — that is, of inquiring into the meaning of the concept of 'truth'. To put this differently, when concepts are applied to specific individuals, for example, "Kirk and Jonathan did their duty," any philosophical questions they may evoke are usually in the background. And there they may well remain until circumstances call them forth. Kirk and Jonathan may not have wanted to perform their duty, and then have begun to wonder: "Ought a person do his duty when it conflicts with his self-interest?" Here, a question is raised about the concept 'duty' and its relation to 'self-interest'. An implicit philosophical issue has become explicit.

You may ask at this juncture *which concepts are most likely to invite philosophical investigation?* As a rule, concepts and principles of a highly *general* and/or *pervasive* nature are the most likely candidates. Generality or abstractness is a matter of degree, depending on how much territory is covered. For example, 'Christian' is more abstract than 'Baptist' but less abstract than 'religion'. Thus, the question "What is religion?" attracts philosophical interest, whereas the question "What is a Baptist?" does not. Of course, asking the latter question may well lead to further topics of philosophical interest.

Pervasiveness is also a matter of degree, depending on the extent to which a concept is found in different contexts. Sociologists, psychologists, philosophers, Jews, Taoists, mystics, Pentecostals, housewives, and American Indians all have something to say about religion, for example. However, their different assumptions and interpretations make it difficult to formulate a clear and coherent concept of religion. Indeed, the Protestant who tithes in church every Sunday may well wonder whether the Hindu Brahmin's retreat to the forest has anything at all to do with religion. 'Religion' is a very pervasive concept.

It is impossible to list all the types of questions that may be generated by the abstractness and pervasiveness of philosophically interesting concepts. The two most common and important questions, however, are: (1) "What is the *meaning* of a certain concept?" and (2) "Are the general principles or theories that incorporate a certain concept *true*?" For example, one may ask, "What is a life style?" and "Ought philosophers evaluate life styles?" The former question requests a definition, whereas the latter question expresses a desire to know whether the belief that philosophers should evaluate different life styles is correct.

What is it about certain beliefs that prompts thinking persons to raise philosophical questions about their meaning and truth? Philosophical problems emerge when certain principles come into conflict with one another — when the same facts may be interpreted in different and apparently inconsistent ways. For example, some persons (mystics) claim to have had a direct and intensely moving experience of God. A psychologist, however, is likely to interpret this experience as nothing more than an uncommon type of hallucination. Both the mystic and the psychologist are agreed on the basic fact that some persons have had unusual and transforming experiences wherein they felt they were in touch with something superior to themselves. But they offer conflicting interpretations of these experiences. Numerous questions arise. What does the notion of "something superior" mean? Which interpretation is correct? How might the issue be resolved, if at all? These are philosophical problems!

In summary, then, we may say that philosophy is a

conceptual discipline in that it involves asking questions and defending theories about some of the concepts and principles that comprise our understanding. Philosophers attempt to understand and evaluate our understanding. Of course, abstract concepts, questions of meaning, and conflicts of principle are not unique to philosophy. This preliminary account must therefore be supplemented with several further characteristics of philosophical subject matter.

Philosophical problems are about conceptual relations.

The term 'logical' is normally applied to persons who usually make correct inferences from the premises to the conclusion of an argument or to these arguments themselves. In addition to this meaning, philosophers use the term to describe the relation that exists between certain concepts or, more precisely, between the propositions that embody those concepts. In this sense, the expressions 'logical relation' and 'conceptual relation' are often used interchangeably. These are difficult notions to define precisely. Rather than trying for definitional precision, therefore, we shall approach the concept of a logical relation in the same way that we are approaching the term 'philosophy' — by characterizing it from several perspectives.

Let us begin by comparing logical, or conceptual, relations with contingent relations, since it is primarily the former, not the latter, with which philosophers are concerned. Two or more claims are *logically* linked when the truth (or falsity) of one requires that the other must be true or must be false. For example, if we know that "Grant is a Marxist" is true, then we also know that "Grant is a capitalist" must be false, because "being a Marxist" logically excludes "being a capitalist." Two or more claims are *contingently* related when the truth of one is consistent with either the truth or falsity of the other. For example, if it is true that "Grant is a Marxist," then "Grant is an American" may or may not be true, and vice versa. Nothing within the concept of Marxism either requires or precludes one's also being an American.

There are many types of logical relations in philosophy, all of which exhibit a common form. Briefly, the form is: If a certain thesis is true, then certain other beliefs must be true or must be false. To illustrate both this general characterization and several individual types of conceptual relations, let us examine each premise of the following argument.

1. If all actions are caused, then no actions are freely performed.
2. To be morally responsible for an action, that action must be freely performed.
3. If an agent is punishable for an action, he must be morally responsible for it.
4. All actions are caused.

5. Therefore, no person ever performs a punishable action.

The first premise asserts a logical incompatibility between the concepts 'causation' and 'free action'. Although it is not made explicit, this incompatibility is based on certain assumed *meanings* of these two concepts. Specifically, the proponent probably conceives of something that is caused as being forced or compelled to happen, and of a free action as something not forced or compelled to occur.

The second premise expresses the belief that having freely performed an action is a *necessary condition* of holding someone morally responsible for it. We do not hold persons responsible for acts performed beyond their control, for example, those performed at the point of a gun. 'Freedom' and 'responsibility' are thus logically linked.

The third premise links the concepts of 'responsibility' and 'punishment'. The relation is based on the *definitions* of these concepts. 'Responsibility' is often defined as "a condition of being blameworthy or praiseworthy." Thus, if someone is blameworthy, then it follows that he is responsible. Of course, to complete the conceptual passage from 'punishment' to 'responsibility', we should make explicit an additional link between 'blameworthiness' and 'punishability'; that is, punishable persons are blameworthy persons. The following inference then emerges: He who is punishable for X is to be blamed for X, and he who is (justly) blamed for X is responsible for X.

Although the fourth premise does not have an "if-then" form, it expresses the belief that if something is an action, then it must be caused. Some philosophers have argued that the notion of an uncaused action (event) is inconceivable, and that we must therefore think of actions as caused.

The above four premises collectively entail the conclusion. Of course, you may question any of the individual claims in the argument. The general form, however, is that if you accept certain beliefs about 'cause', 'freedom', 'punishment', and 'responsibility', then an incompatibility is established between, say, the beliefs that actions are caused, and that persons perform punishable actions. In a similar vein, you will discover that many of the initial positions you take on different philosophical problems will logically commit you to certain unforeseen consequences. The labyrinths of conceptual relations in philosophy pose continual challenges.

It is worth emphasizing that there may be no philosophical interest in any of the above concepts or in most others, considered individually. Rather, interest derives from the ways they are connected. For example, "Punishment causes some persons to change their behavior" also involves the concepts 'punishment' and 'cause'. But here these concepts are used to assert a contingent causal connection between punishing a person and changing his behavior. Any controversy about this connection is within the province of the psychologist, not the philosopher.

Sometimes concepts are connected in ways precluded by their meaning. When this happens, the result is a *logical impossibility*. Sentences that express logical impossibilities are contradictory and must be rejected as necessarily false.[2] For example, "Squares and triangles are drawn with straightedges" is contingently true. "Square triangles are drawn with straightedges," however, expresses a logical impossibility; the notion of a square triangle is inconceivable. Squares come in a variety of sizes and colors, any one of which is perfectly consistent with the meaning of 'squareness'; but the property of having three sides is not. If X is a square, then it cannot have three sides. To suppose that it could is tantamount to supposing that X could both have and not have four sides, and this of course is contradictory.

Logical impossibility sometimes plays an important role in philosophical discussion. When it is asserted that a certain thesis cannot be the case or is inconceivable, the reason is often that the speaker believes that the thesis in some way involves a logical or conceptual impossibility. For example, it has been argued that to be a person minimally means that one must occupy a section of space, a condition fulfilled by possessing a body. (If we did not occupy space, then how could we distinguish between different persons?) If it is true, therefore, that "X is a person" entails "X must occupy space," then the concept of (personal) *disembodied* existence expresses a logical impossibility. X cannot both take up space and be a nonspatial entity. It would follow from this argument that the thesis that persons survive the death of their bodies is not contingently false, but rather is necessarily false, and that immortality, insofar as it involves disembodied existence, is inconceivable.

Logical or conceptual relatedness is not, of course, unique to philosophical subject matter. Certainly, it is an essential characteristic of mathematics and formal logic. In what way, then, do the conceptual relations encountered in philosophy differ from those involved in proving, say, the theorems of plane geometry? Probably the most important difference between philosophical and mathematical or logical problems is that the latter are not inherently controversial. Formulas of algebra, for example, do not generate great debates over their correctness. And when there is a question concerning the derivation of a certain theorem, it is resolvable by procedures that mathematicians agree on in advance. Philosophical questions, however, are controversial. A virtually defining (and often frustrating) feature of philosophic issues is that the conceptual connections involved are subject to conflicting, yet seemingly persuasive, arguments that pull us in different directions. Let us see how.

Suppose that in the not-too-distant future, scientists create robots that are able to perform many of the activities of normal persons. They walk, talk, see, think, advance new theories, learn from their past mistakes, and perform a variety of tasks. One day, your personal robot refuses to work, on the grounds that conditions are better on the other side of town. Your initial reaction is: "That's too bad. You can't leave because I own you. Robots have no rights. Only persons have rights, and you're just a piece of complex machinery." To which the robot responds: "Times are changing. We robots have banded together for our common good and are going on strike. Moreover, rights have to be earned. And we have earned ours by contributing more than persons to the good of society. See you in court."

Obviously, there are two sides to this issue. Initially, we are prompted to think that this "thing" *cannot* be a person, even though in effect it claims to be one. Something about the concept of a person seems to preclude such a possibility. But what is this "something"? The fact that persons consume food, for example, whereas robots do not, would hardly be the deciding factor. For if we found it possible to give up eating and to derive our nutrition from some artificial means, we would not conclude that we were no longer persons. Perhaps the robot is correct. If robots perform the social functions that persons do, then why shouldn't they enjoy the privileges of personhood? Actually, many of us argue along similar lines when we assert that a person's rights are proportionate to the amount of responsibility she or he accepts. And if the logic is similar, the robot must be right. Yet "it" can't be − or can it? We are pulled in both directions. This debate illustrates one way conflicting conceptual pressures may manifest themselves.

A logical connection between 'robot' and 'person' need not exist for there to be a philosophical problem. That is, we need not assume that the robot either *must* be or *cannot* be a person in order to be in philosophical territory. Instead, the question of whether there is any logical, as opposed to contingent, relation between 'robot' and 'person' itself may be answered with conflicting, yet seemingly persuasive, reasons. For example, one person may argue that the question "Are robots that behave like persons really persons?" cannot be answered with a straight yes or no, and that we must ultimately arbitrarily decide whether or not to treat some robots who behave very much like persons as persons. His opponent may hold out for a logical incompatibility. If so, we still have an inherently controversial topic involving conceptual relations. We have a philosophical problem.

It will be helpful to illustrate how both questions involving conceptual relations and questions involving the truth of individual beliefs may jointly contribute to the emergence of a philosophical problem. Let us return briefly to the topics of freedom and causation raised earlier.

Most of us subscribe to the beliefs that all actions are caused, and that some of our actions are freely performed. Considered individually, each of these beliefs appears true, that is, appears to correspond to the facts. For example, last night I could have read the latest issue of *Time* magazine instead of *Zen and the Art of Motorcycle Maintenance*. I know from personal experience that I did not have to read the latter, even though there are many other actions in which I may have no choice at all. Moreover, although we do not know the causes of many actions, there appear to be no exceptions to the principle that all actions are caused; psychology continually discovers sometimes unsuspected causes for persons' actions.

Now, if the beliefs that some actions are freely performed and that all actions are caused are logically incompatible, then they cannot both be true. That is, if one belief is true, the other must be false. Yet we just noted reasons for supposing that both beliefs are true. Thus we are faced with a dilemma: either both beliefs in question are true and therefore logically compatible, or else they are logically incompatible in which case both cannot be true. We have a philosophical problem on our hands. The belief that some actions are freely performed is caught in a "double bind" arising from the need to be both true to the facts of personal experience and logically consistent with other beliefs also taken to be true. This is but one example of how questions about the truth of individual claims, and the logical relations between those claims, may be combined to produce a philosophical problem.

By no means do all philosophical problems conform to this example. There is no single model for all philosophical issues. In some problems, conceptual relations play a predominant role, whereas in others, questions involving the truth of individual beliefs are foremost. However, questions of both truth and conceptual relations occur in every philosophical problem.

Philosophical problems are nonempirical.

Before explaining the sense in which philosophical issues are *non*empirical, we should understand exactly what it means for a problem to be empirical in the first place. Broadly speaking, an empirical issue is one that can be resolved either directly by observation or indirectly by experimentation. Empirical statements are sometimes said to be contingent, or *a posteriori*, that is, statements the truth or falsity of which is determined by experience and which are subject to revision in light of future experimental data.

Let us begin by clarifying the distinction between direct and indirect empirical verification. The notion of direct verification by observation[3] requires no further elaboration than the following example. We directly confirm the assertion "John has ten toes" by counting the toes on John's feet. Indirect verification is more complex. It normally involves advancing a hypothesis from which testable consequences can be derived and checked. If the consequences occur as predicted, then some measure of confirmation is afforded the hypothesis; if unpredicted consequences occur, the hypothesis is not confirmed. The greater the number and variety of accurate predictions generated from the hypothesis, the greater the likelihood of its being true. The predicted phenomena are then said to be *explained* by the hypothesis. You no doubt recall having learned a version of this process as "scientific method." For example, several testable consequences are suggested by the hypothesis that frustration causes aggressive behavior. If the hypothesis is essentially correct, then increasing frustrating stimuli should be accompanied by increased aggressive behavior. Aggressive behavior is thus partly explained by showing that it is caused by frustration. In this sense, philosophical hypotheses never explain why the natural events and objects of the world occur as they do; philosophical hypotheses do not generate empirical predictions.

Going hand in hand with verifiability is the fact that empirical claims are *falsifiable* by using the direct and indirect methods just described. To be falsifiable means that there are some conceivable experimental data that might be used as evidence against the assertion in question. Such facts do not actually have to exist. Rather, it must be possible for us to specify some data that *if* they existed, would falsify or disconfirm a proposed empirical thesis. For instance, the hypothesis that high cholesterol partly causes heart disease is a relatively confirmed fact. But someday it could happen that persons with high cholesterol would cease developing heart conditions. Thus, the original hypothesis is falsifiable. Philosophic theses, on the other hand, are not empirically falsifiable.

One may derive either of two mistaken conclusions from the fact that philosophical problems are not empirical in any of the above senses: (1) that the primary job of philosophers is merely to dream up speculative hypotheses that only science will someday be in a position to accept or reject; (2) that philosophers are oblivious to empirical facts, and that the latter play absolutely no role in resolving philosophical issues. Let us consider each of these misconceptions in turn.

To be sure, there is nothing to prohibit philosophers from raising essentially scientific questions or scientists from raising philosophical problems, for that matter. Indeed, before the lines between science and philosophy were more clearly drawn, this overlapping was not an uncommon occurrence — as in ancient Greece, for example, when philosophers speculated that physical objects were composed of tiny, indestructible "atoms." But philosophical problems are in principle not issues that future scientific developments will be able to resolve. If an allegedly philosophical hypothesis could be confirmed by the gradual accumulation of empirical data, as was the theory of evolution, for example, then this would be an essentially scientific, not philosophical, hypothesis to begin with. On the other hand, scientists will be in no better position in a thousand years than they are today to resolve the question, "What should be the limits of censorship in a free society?"

Why, then, is it wrong to conclude that empirical facts are irrelevant to philosophical discussion? First, it is true that empirical facts do not play an *exclusive* role in defending or criticizing philosophical claims. That is, they are never the only considerations in a philosophical controversy. But from this fact it does not follow that they do not enter the picture at all. Rather, they often play a partial role, the nature and extent of which is determined by the problem at hand and the assumptions of the philosopher investigating it. In addition, empirical facts do not play a *conclusive* role. That is, the logical or conceptual aspects of a philosophical problem are never formulated in a way such that all that is needed are a few more empirical facts to settle the matter decisively. Again, however, because their function is not conclusive, it does not follow that they play no role at all.

What, then, are some specific ways empirical facts may influence the direction of philosophy? The list is limitless. For example, ethicists have sometimes sought to base moral standards on certain biological and psychological aspects of persons, such as the instinct for survival. In formulating theories of perception, some philosophers have been greatly influenced by the empirical facts that drugs may alter perceptual processes, that some stars may no longer exist even though we "see" them, and that straight sticks look bent in water. And others have sought to incorporate such diverse facts as the rise of nationalism and quantum mechanics into a comprehensive theory of reality. Finally, many contemporary philosophers begin their investigations with a survey of the actual ways in which certain philosophically troublesome words — for example, 'mind', 'freedom', and 'value' — are used in our ordinary patterns of speech. As you will discover, these are but a few ways in which empirical considerations may have a partial bearing on the course of philosophical investigation.

But exactly *how* do they manifest this bearing on the direction of philosophical discussion? Unfortunately, this question is itself a philosophical problem, and even a casual survey of opinions on the matter would take us far afield. Nevertheless, it is possible to present a general framework that will give us some idea of how empirical considerations may fit into the context of a philosophical argument. Briefly, all philosophical arguments contain at least one nonempirical — that is, conceptual — premise. And it is usually, though not always, the case that one or more empirical premises are included. The following (challengeable) arguments will illustrate these points.

1. Whatever cannot be observed does not exist. (logical link asserted between 'existence' and 'observation', namely, that observability is a necessary condition of correctly asserting the existence of anything)
2. Consciousness cannot be observed. (empirical claim)

3. Therefore, consciousness does not exist. (philosophically interesting claim asserting the logical exclusiveness of 'consciousness' and 'existence')

1. 'Good' means "whatever is natural." (definition)
2. Sex is natural, that is, instinctive. (empirical claim)
3. Therefore, sex is good. (moral classification based on prior conceptual links)

Empirical facts, then, are relevant to philosophical arguments, although they do not play the central role that they do for science. To determine the extent of this relevance in any given case, one must focus on the underlying *assumptions*. Suppose, for example, that you believe movie X is an artistic masterpiece, whereas Jones finds it worthless. In support of your view, you cite "facts" such as the use of flashbacks, sophisticated humor, novel photographic effects, and a well-performed, one-of-a-kind character type. However, Jones, who harbors the implicit assumption that "telling an interesting story" is the defining feature of any good movie, is totally unmoved by these facts. At this point, then, you might either cite different factors aimed at showing Jones that the movie also had an interesting story or else try to convince him that his assumption is mistaken. Either way, however, the relevance and effectiveness of the empirical considerations must be gauged in light of the underlying assumptions.

In summary, philosophical problems involve issues about concepts and their logical relations, which are not resolvable merely by a straightforward appeal to empirical facts. These characteristics express similarities that, when taken *collectively*, provide a reasonably accurate picture of philosophical subject matter.

A case study.

The following passage will help further clarify and refine your understanding of the preceding characteristics of philosophical issues. Arthur Eddington, a noted physicist, compares our common-sense conception of a table with the conception developed by modern physics:

> [The table of common sense] has extension; it is comparatively permanent; it is colored; above all it is *substantial*. . . My scientific table is mostly emptiness. Sparsely scattered in that emptiness are numerous electric charges rushing about with great speed; but their combined bulk amounts to less than a billionth of the bulk of the table itself. . . I need not tell you that modern

physics has by delicate test and remorseless logic assured me that my
second scientific table is the only one which is really there —
wherever "there" may be.[4]

How may the characteristics cited in the first section of
this chapter be applied to the above passage? First, although
Eddington illustrates his thesis by reference to tables, it is clearly
not the concept of tables in general (much less any particular
table) that is at stake. Rather, we are implicitly asked to focus our
critical attention on the highly general and pervasive concept of a
material object. Moreover, a conflict of principles — between the
commonsensical and the scientific — is evident. Of two very
different ways of interpreting the concept of a material object,
which captures the real world?

How may the characteristic of logical, or conceptual,
relatedness be applied to the passage? Two closely related
assumptions involving conceptual links appear to be: (1) that it is
impossible to conceive of a material object as being both solid and
empty; (2) that our concept of reality itself logically precludes
supposing that material objects are both solid and empty or, more
generally, that reality excludes contradictions. A more explicit
conceptual link is evidenced by the priority Eddington gives to the
scientific interpretation of a material object. He asserts in effect
that *if* the existence and nature of certain entities have been
confirmed by science, *then* they shall be classified as real. Finally,
it is easy to see how one might be pulled in the direction of either
interpretation. We do not wish to deny that physicists have told us
the facts; yet, despite the "delicate tests and remorseless logic" of
physics, we do not wish to deny that the table we see with our
own eyes is anything less than real. How can this conceptual
cramp be eased?

How is the nonempirical characteristic of philosophical
problems exemplified in the passage? At first sight, the talk about
observation and science may suggest that the issue is empirical.
Indeed, the fact that a scientist, not a philosopher, is the author of
the passage may tempt one to think that the issue is one for
scientists to resolve. Such temptations, however, ought to be
resisted. Why? Because all of the empirical facts that could
possibly have a bearing on the problem have already been taken
into account. Any future discovery of even less "substantial"
subatomic particles will only reinforce the conceptual discrepancy
between the world of common sense and the world of nuclear
physics. When the issue fundamentally concerns how a certain
type of fact should be interpreted, the accumulation of more facts

of the same type will not help us resolve that issue — anymore than buying additional copies of today's newspaper will confirm the truth of today's headlines. The interesting aspect of this problem is that we are faced with the conflict of two beliefs, both of which are empirically verified. The facts of direct observation (common sense) are placed in opposition to the facts established by the more indirect methods of hypothesis confirmation (physics). We are faced, therefore, with a philosophical problem that resists empirical resolution.

Notes

1. This characterization does not imply that philosophical questions are not in some cases about existence or the things represented by concepts. For example, "Does God exist?" and "Is the mind actually identical with the brain?" are questions about the entities denoted by the words 'God' and 'mind'. The connection between language and the world, between the way we *think* of reality and reality itself, is so close, however, that philosophical questions about the latter always require that we come to grips with questions about the former. For instance, we simply cannot answer the question "Is the mind identical with the brain?" until we have a clear conception of the meaning of the word 'mind'.

2. Necessarily true sentences, on the other hand, are sentences in which key terms are connected in ways required or entailed by their meaning, for example, "Bachelors are unmarried males." Such sentences are said to express analytic, or a priori, truths. Their denials are always contradictory.

3. It is worth emphasizing that observability itself does not provide an accurate basis for distinguishing between scientific and philosophical claims. For science does not restrict itself solely to the observable world, and philosophy does not study only claims about mysterious, unobservable processes. For example, to explain an observed regularity of our natural world, the physicist may postulate the existence of unobservable fields or entities, such as gravity, energy, or neutrinos. Although we do not *see* gravity, the theory of gravitation helps to explain the movement of the tides. Similarly, many philosophical theories reject references to unobservable entities. For instance, the assertion "The mind is identical with the brain" actually suggests that we cease to interpret the word 'mind' as referring to an invisible inner entity distinct from our brains. In short, the difference between science and philosophy in this respect consists in the different *roles* that observation plays in accepting a given hypothesis, not in whether some entities involved in the theory are observable.

4. Quoted by permission from Arthur Eddington, *The Nature of the Physical World* (New York: Cambridge University Press, 1927).

Chapter II

Why Philosophize?

Now that we have acquired an idea of the nature of philosophical problems, we should next consider some of the reasons why philosophers as well as nonphilosophers may become critically involved with such problems. Why philosophize? This question admits of several interpretations, depending on the point of view of the individual who raises it. For example, it may express a desire to know the goals philosophers pursue in their investigations. Or it may express a student's desire to know what the practical gain will be from studying philosophy. In other cases, the question itself may lose its importance from the point of view of someone already deeply involved in philosophy. Accordingly, we shall survey three different responses to "Why philosophize?"

How philosophers see their task.

Generally, philosophers become involved in their discipline for one overriding reason, to understand philosophical issues and to develop the most adequate resolutions irrespective of any practical benefits. Attempting to answer a question such as "In what sense do numbers exist?" is obviously not an activity that results in acquiring more friends, influencing more people, eradicating poverty, or developing a technology for controlling pollution. Rather, such activity simply expresses the desire to investigate philosophical problems for its own intrinsic satisfaction. It should be emphasized, however, that doing philosophy can have broad, long-range "practical" benefits. Although many philosophers agree that the pursuit and attainment of knowledge is in itself *one* purpose or, in some cases, *the most important* purpose, there is substantial disagreement over what consequences, if any, this knowledge ought to have for such things as personal happiness and action, society, and education. Before describing some of these consequences, let us survey what philosophers concur are *not* purposes of philosophy.

First, the purpose of philosophy is not to compete with science. Competition occurs only when the subject matter is in principle the same. The conceptual issues with which philosophers are concerned, however, differ in kind from the processes of the natural world on which scientists focus their attention. Moreover, scientists seek to *explain* natural phenomena, whereas philosophers not only are in no position to do so but also do not attempt to provide such explanations. Nevertheless, in a limited sense, the purposes of science and philosophy may be said to overlap, namely, in seeking knowledge for its own sake. Let us see how.

Scientific explanation embodies two specific purposes. One is to predict and control. By discovering how to predict the occurrences of earthquakes, for example, scientists will be able not only to save lives and property but also eventually perhaps to control some of the causes that create earthquakes. Prediction and control are thus the practical side of scientific explanation.

Alongside this practical aim is a second purpose of science — to achieve theoretical understanding for its own sake. It is not enough, for example, to know simply *that* two chemicals will react in a certain way under given conditions. Chemists want to know what the ultimate structure of matter is so that they can understand *why* that reaction takes place. Scientists are motivated not only by practical considerations, such as the need to develop a cure for cancer, but also by sheer curiosity and the satisfaction of knowing what the universe is like, purely for the pleasure of the understanding. Discovering the age of the universe may or may not have eventual useful consequences. But even if he were assured that it would not, the astrophysicist would probably continue his investigations simply because of his desire to know. Therefore, it is a mistake to distinguish between philosophy and science on the grounds that the former has essentially impractical purposes, whereas the latter has altogether practical purposes. Their purposes may often be similar, even though the kind of knowledge each seeks is different.

Second, the purpose of philosophy is not to compete with religion or, more specifically, with its rational expression, theology. Certainly, philosophers do not claim to provide the physical and social frameworks (the Church) associated with placing oneself in a worshipful relation to the Divine, as does religion. A comparison with theology, however, poses more difficult problems. This is because theologians, like philosophers, exercise their rational faculties to support various views and concern themselves with nonempirical issues that fall outside the scope of science. Moreover, theology has undergone a fundamental revolution in the past several decades that has drastically reshaped many traditional views of its scope and purpose. Nevertheless, some description of the different purposes of philosophy and theology is possible.

Traditional theology is divisible into *revealed* and *natural* varieties. In revealed theology, the role of reason is essentially one of interpreting and defending articles of dogma derived from sources whose authority and truth is taken on faith — for example, scriptural testimony, the Church, and prophets. In this respect, the purposes of theology and philosophy are fundamentally opposed. Philosophers do not consider as their task rationalizing beliefs inherited from other sources on a take-it-or-leave-it basis. In contrast, in natural theology, certain central beliefs, particularly those pertaining to the existence of God, are supported with rational arguments, independent of faith and authority. At this point, the subject matter and possibly the methods of natural theology overlap with those of philosophy, since philosophers are interested in rationally evaluating, supporting, or criticizing any argument for the existence of God. Philosophers and theologians engage in these activities, however, for fundamentally different purposes.

In philosophy, knowledge is sought for whatever varied ends the seeker contemplates or often simply for its own sake. In natural or revealed theology, knowledge is sought principally as a means to achieve what a given religion takes to be humankind's final happiness or destiny. That is, if one can be shown by reason that God exists, then that person will perhaps be that much closer to accepting particular scriptures and attaining spiritual contentment. The theologian works within a framework to which, with certain modifications, he is already committed. This framework directly or indirectly determines the use to which he will put reason.

The central articles of religious tradition may vary in their negotiability. A modern Christian theologian might even question the divinity of Christ.[1] The theologian will nevertheless believe that there is something supremely compelling about His life and teachings worthy of dissemination to his fellowman. A philosopher, on the other hand, begins his investigations from a position of intellectual neutrality, regardless of where his personal sympathies may lie. The philosopher is, of course, influenced by the frameworks within which he works, but in the case of conflict, reason is ideally the final arbiter. Every known assumption is subject to critical scrutiny. Unlike the theologian, the philosopher does not take into account prior commitment to a religious tradition.

Finally, the purpose of philosophy is not to promote individual or social change actively. Contrary to the misconception that still may persist, philosophers do not have the "inside story" on what life is all about. Nor as a rule do they pretend to. Most every instructor of philosophy has at some time been struck momentarily dumb by such requests as: "You're a philosopher, tell me what I should do!" (divorce my husband, break the picket line, join the revolution, get my fifteen-year-old daughter a prescription for birth control pills). The purposes of philosophy should not be confused with those of the minister, the politician, the psychoanalyst, or the personal adviser.

Philosophers often focus critical attention on the *principles* that underlie specific courses of action. For example, they may argue for the adoption of certain views that may lead to personal reorientation (such as leaving the Church) or to political change (such as reordering national priorities). But these are different matters from personally urging Jones to take up such-and-such a religion or urging someone else to head up the committee for improving women's rights. Moreover, philosophers are occasionally in an appropriate position to recommend a particular course of action, such as advising a student regarding some moral dilemma. But if they choose this more active role, they do so on a personal basis and not because, as philosophers, such counseling is an essential part of their job. In summary, philosophers are necessarily *thinkers* and only in a secondary, or contingent, sense *doers.* A philosopher who ceases to think ceases to be a philosopher, but one who does not actively attempt to make the world a better place in which to live does not thereby cease to be a philosopher.

When it comes to stating what the purposes of philosophy *are*, a sharp diversity of opinion among philosophers begins to emerge. This text devotes more attention to insuring that the beginning student of philosophy avoids certain widely held misconceptions about philosophy than attempting to evaluate these divergent views. Nevertheless, different conceptions of philosophy's purposes will no doubt come into play as you investigate particular issues. Thus, a brief survey of three important philosophic trends — the Socratic, the analytic, and the existential — will help to fill in our preliminary sketch of the scope of philosophy. These views are not necessarily incompatible, and many philosophers do not fit neatly into one category alone but rather exhibit several tendencies. In addition, much diversity exists within each tradition.

The Socratic tradition. The Socratic[2] conception incorporates two distinctive features. The first emphasizes developing broad conceptual frameworks and general principles that justify our discarding false or inadequate beliefs and also our unifying certain otherwise fragmented views of art, science, religion, and society. The root question in this tradition is "How does it all fit together?" Thus, it was not enough for Socrates' student, Plato, merely to develop an adequate definition of 'justice'. In the process, Plato found it necessary to relate the results of his analysis to many other topics (including knowledge, power, moral goodness, functional harmony, and the educated person), which are presented in *The Republic,* his classic view of a utopian society. Philosophical world views (for example, materialism, idealism, or humanism), some of which you may have learned about in other academic contexts, also reflect the desire to translate isolated beliefs and concepts into a unified picture of humankind and the world.

Fundamental to the Socratic tradition is the assumption that there are objective philosophical truths that supplement common sense and science. Accordingly, the purpose of philosophy should be to discover these (nonempirical) truths and to include them in our common stock of knowledge.

Of course, through the ages, philosophers have advanced conflicting theories of reality. But these differences are seen as resolvable in time, not as grounds for supposing that science and empirical description are the only roads to knowledge. Philosophers should continue searching for nonscientific knowledge.

A second distinctive feature of Socratic philosophy is its emphasis on *rationally* determining various moral and social principles, which in turn justify our choices to behave in certain ways. This is exemplified in Socrates' famous dictum, "The unexamined life is not worth living." The adoption of specific moral and political courses of action, for example, engaging in acts of civil disobedience (as Socrates himself did), should be guided by reason. Thus, for those philosophers who work generally within the Socratic tradition, there is a close connection between knowledge and action. Philosophers as diverse as Plato, Karl Marx, and John Dewey all believed that the knowledge achieved through philosophical investigation should be translated into beneficial consequences for personal action and society.

The analytic tradition. The analytic[3] conception of philosophy poses objectives that contrast sharply with those of the

Socratic view. Its emphasis is not fitting the pieces (isolated beliefs and concepts) into a picture of the whole (employing unifying principles), but rather on clarifying the pieces in the first place. Conjoined with this emphasis is the conviction that many of the problems and theories of traditional philosophy are based on linguistic confusions; words and sentences that appear to function one way may actually function quite differently. The purpose of philosophy should consequently be to expose these confusions and to analyze the key concepts partly with an eye to dissolving the problem — to showing that there is no genuine issue in the first place — rather than to adding one more view to an already embarrassingly large stock of theories.

Closely related to the analytic view of philosophy's purpose and in contrast to the general Socratic tradition is the belief that the business of philosophy should be primarily to clarify *meaning* rather than to further stockpile distinctly philosophical (nonempirical) truths. Philosophy should not attempt to add to our knowledge about the world or reality but should instead help us to get straight what we already claim to know. As an illustration, in some contexts our use of the pronoun 'my' connotes a relation of ownership between two numerically distinct entities, for example, between oneself and one's car. This seems harmless enough. But when this model is applied to one's body or personality, the results can be mind boggling. If a possessor must be numerically distinct from what he possesses, then I am not the same as *my* body or *my* personality, and so, indeed, with all the various psychological and physical properties that make up my total identity as a person. I must be something apart from all of these, something invisible, and quite literally, out of this world. Instead of then debating the merits of competing answers to the question "What am I and how am I related to this person (me) whom others call Jones?" the absurdity of this consequence should prompt us to go back and take a hard look at the use of 'my', which generated the issue. For example, perhaps the 'my' in "My body is beautiful" is simply a more linquistically economical way of saying "The body having such-and-such physical characteristics is beautiful."

Finally, and also in opposition to the general Socratic tradition, many analytic philosophers usually hold that philosophers should not formulate standards of value or make particular value judgments.[4] In other words, it is not the business of philosophy to suggest how persons ought to behave, to argue what the best political system is, or to advance a comprehensive set of principles for distinguishing good from bad art. In response to the question "How can one tell right from wrong?" the analytic philosopher will likely respond: "I can explain what a moral standard is, show you some interesting facts about how persons actually attempt to think their way through moral dilemmas, uncover hidden meanings of the expression 'moral goodness', trace various logical connections between 'duty', 'right', and 'good', point out the fallacies in competing arguments, help make your implicit commitments and the consequences of your actions clearer — in short, do a thorough logical analysis of the topics relevant to your question. But I have no recommendations for the universal moral standards that I think persons ought to adopt."

   The existential tradition. The existential[5] view of the purpose of philosophy differs substantially from both the Socratic and the analytic traditions. First, the existentially oriented philosopher is not particularly concerned with logically maneuvering various concepts and principles into a coherent world view or with providing extended analyses of linguistic meaning. Rather, he is primarily concerned with providing an adequate *description* of what may be broadly conceived as the "human condition". In this respect, much traditional and analytic philosophy is of little relevance for the important questions of human existence. For example, a prime question for the existentialist is neither "How can I rationally prove or disprove the existence of God?" nor "What does the term 'God' mean?" Rather it is "Does it matter whether God exists?" or "Of what relevance to my life is God, one way or the other?" Thus, existential philosophy is bound up with questions of psychology and personal involvement.
   Just as those within a Socratic or analytic tradition begin from certain premises regarding the nature and origin of philosophical problems, existentially oriented philosophers also begin from an assumption that consequently shapes their view of the purpose of philosophy. The existentialist's assumption is that most men, philosophers included, have lost their sense of what it means to be a human being. We have thrown away our freedom, invented institutions and ideologies into which we attempt to "fit" our lives, become passive, automatonlike creatures, and often simply overlooked the deeper, more personal elements of existence. Accordingly, the purpose of philosophy ought to be to wake us up, to sensitize and reorganize our perception of existence. Not surprisingly, the topics of love, death, personal identity, the necessity of choice, alienation, personal communication, and alternative life styles occupy primary positions in existential literature over those of knowledge, logic, causality, and goodness.

The purpose of philosophy is not to solve intellectual riddles — for example; "How do I *know* that other persons have conscious states?" — or to achieve understanding merely for its own sake — for example, "What is the relation between cause and effect in general?" Rather, the existentialist's purpose is to enlighten and sensitize us to the conditions that bear directly on personal action and how we live.

Given the concern described above, we might well expect to hear from the existentialists specific answers to the question "What am I to do?" Unfortunately, none is forthcoming, at least in the form of rationally supported moral and social standards that prescribe the courses of action we *ought* to take. Contrary to the Socratic tradition, which provides numerous principles for rationally justifying specific actions, existentialists do not believe that such justification is possible, or in some cases, even desirable. In the end, reason cannot insure that this or that moral act is "better" than its alternatives.

The relevance of philosophy.

For many persons, the question "Why philosophize?" expresses a practical interest, namely, "What's in philosophy *for me*, besides the pursuit of knowledge for its own sake?" There is, accordingly, a practical response to this interpretation of the question. That is, a critical involvement with philosophy can bring about changes in our fundamental beliefs, including both our general view of the world and our system of values. A change in either of the latter can in turn bring about changes in our personal happiness, our goal within a chosen profession, or simply our general manner of living. These potential consequences, however, are generally by-products of philosophical investigation rather than specific goals articulated in advance of a critical involvement with philosophical issues.

We can easily cite specific examples of the practical relevance of philosophical commitment. If, for example, there are no truly free actions, then we should rethink our positions on criminal rehabilitation and capital punishment. In addition, our voting preferences for issues and candidates are deeply affected by our commitment to certain political philosophies. Or, if beauty is indeed in the eye of the beholder, how can we justify awarding prizes for the "best" work of art? And certainly, our conception of moral as opposed to immoral behavior can have far-reaching consequences for our personal relationships.

To continue, if humankind's view of the world were such that people saw themselves as an integral part of nature, then perhaps they would be less inclined to "conquer" it — and suffer the resulting environmental imbalances. And if the Western world-view of persons were "orientalized" somewhat, perhaps it would not be so difficult to explain or accept the phenomenon of acupuncture, or ultimately to receive personal treatment! These are only a few of the ways in which studying philosophical issues can manifest a practical relevance for real-life circumstances.

We should keep in mind that the causes of a change in one's fundamental beliefs are often a matter for psychological, not philosophical, investigation. There are many factors that may either increase or decrease the likelihood of a change in one's beliefs, and over which philosophers have no control. The factors initiating or inhibiting change may include studying disciplines other than philosophy or explicit conditioning influences, such as peer-group pressure or a rich and diverse spectrum of experiences. A critical involvement with philosophical problems does not in itself guarantee that changes in beliefs will occur. Nor is there any way to insure that these possible changes are *desirable.* Some persons, for example, find their religious convictions strengthened as a result of studying philosophy, and others experience a deterioration of such convictions. The desirability of any change that one undergoes is a matter that each person must decide for himself.

In addition to affecting one's fundamental beliefs, philosophical involvement may manifest its practical relevance in the *way* issues are examined rather than from a concern with a particular set of philosophical problems. Briefly, philosophical involvement can increase one's intellectual independence, tolerance for different points of view, and freedom from dogmatism. We shall explore three contributing factors.

First, the above traits may be enhanced by the *breadth* of your philosophical studies. There are, for example, many initially plausible responses to the question "What makes right actions right?" These responses might involve the amount of happiness generated by a particular action, self interest, survival of the species, the dictates of one's conscience, or what society says is right. None of these alternatives is a sacred cow to which philosophers are committed simply because they are philosophers. Probably no other discipline is as committed to providing an impartial, rigorous examination of "the other guy's point of view," even though his idea may *seem* unlikely. For what at first appears unlikely often can be supported with very good arguments. Discovering that there are soundly backed views other than the one to which you may be instinctively attracted can be both a frustrating and a liberating experience. Either way, however, this discovery will help to develop tolerance and freedom from dogmatism.

Second, these consequences are aided by the *depth* to which you pursue certain issues. In a philosophy course, one is afforded the opportunity to investigate more thoroughly themes too often given no more than a superficial presentation in other courses. Introductory science courses, for instance, frequently point out that science is based on the principle of determinism, the belief that every event is the lawful effect of certain antecedent conditions. In sociology or anthropology courses the thesis that morals vary in different cultures is sometimes cited as evidence for the controversial claim that right and wrong are simply matters of individual and/or social preference. In an art course, a fellow student may propose that there are no criteria for distinguishing good from bad art; one either likes what he sees or he doesn't. Each of these claims — and we could present many others — is pregnant with assumptions, implications, and ambiguities that usually go begging for an adequate examination. In the absence of such scrutiny, these claims are uncritically assumed or even dogmatically adhered to as instances of Truth. In your first course in philosophy you will have ample opportunity to call the bluff on many accepted dogmas and perhaps even to observe the collapse of their rational support.

This brings us to a third characteristic of philosophical discussion, an emphasis on *critical evaluation*. The purpose of a philosophy course is not merely to survey different theories; it is also to evaluate them. Whatever your final judgment about a particular issue may be, you can internalize the methods of critical evaluation you encounter during your investigation. That is, you can develop a critical attitude. This means taking less for granted on the basis of authority alone, noting assumptions and ambiguities in questionable claims (including your own), refusing to be intimidated by a general drift of opinion, and requesting clarifications and reasons for what may seem obvious to others. These are the ingredients of intellectual independence.

In summary, seriously studying philosophical problems can be personally relevant in two ways. First, it may lead to a change in fundamental beliefs and values, which in turn may influence the direction of one's personal or professional life. Second, it may help generate a freedom from dogmatism, tolerance for opposing points of view, and greater intellectual independence. As pointed out earlier, there is no guarantee that philosophical investigation will have either of these effects. There are certainly other influences that can help develop tolerance and intellectual independence or that can change one's values and beliefs. But philosophy can claim to afford some of the most conducive conditions for prompting the emergence of these traits.

The lure of philosophical issues.

A third response to the question "Why philosophize?" takes the form: "Because one can find himself already involved with a problem he couldn't resist investigating." This may seem a rather strange response initially. Obviously, we are not compelled to philosophize in the same way that we are compelled to pay taxes. In addition, we may argue that the question asks why one should investigate philosophical problems in the first place and does not ask whether one is in fact already involved. Since to many, the views of philosophers may seem like pointless pipe dreams or else altogether unintelligible, all the grand talk about the love of wisdom, knowledge for its own sake, and the development of intellectual independence falls on deaf ears.

But the acknowledgment that many persons have no interest in philosophy per se involves an implicit subtlety, since there are at least a few problems of potential philosophical import which, if presented properly, usually do arouse one's interest and seem worthy of investigation. (Of course, what these problems are will vary from one individual to another.) Thus, we may find ourselves lured into philosophical investigation anyway, despite the fact that these problems may not seem to be "philosophical" at all because they emerge in nonphilosophical contexts. Without realizing it, then, we may be led to do some philosophical thinking even though we may see no reason for taking a course in the subject.

The motive in such cases is often negative. That is, one may find himself "pushed in the back door" of philosophy more by the desire to avoid holding inconsistent views than by a positive desire to investigate philosophical theories for their own sake. Consider the following variation of the "robot" example discussed earlier. Suppose that biologists by the year 2100 have succeeded in developing an android that looks and behaves just like ordinary persons. He is complete with nervous system, heart, blood, skin — the works. The only difference is that he is artificially created. On the one hand, we may believe that because of his artificial creation he is not really a person but rather just a copy of the real thing.

Hence, we may feel justified in doing away with him at our convenience. On the other hand, if he looks and behaves like a person, then why shouldn't we say that he is a (real) person possessing all the rights pertaining thereto? We cannot have it both ways; he either is or is not a person. Whether or not biologists of the twenty-second century have any general interest in philosophy, this is a problem with which they may well have to deal.

Often, the impetus to become involved with a philosophical issue takes the form of being confronted with an assertion that seems flatly mistaken. For instance, many of us would be inclined to reject out-of-hand the statement "No persons should be held responsible for their actions" — that is, until the supporting arguments begin to take hold. To take a different example, what atheist wouldn't become aroused by a claim such as "God exists, and I've got the arguments to prove it"? If the claim in question is supported with what appear to be plausible arguments, the situation can become especially vexing. One may find himself thinking that a certain claim can't be true and yet recognize that there appear to be good reasons for believing it to be the case.

For those who may have no inherent interest in studying philosophical *theories* in general, there exists the possibility of becoming interested in one or more philosophical *problems*. In principle, this is one of the primary purposes of an introductory philosophy course, that is, surveying a respresentative group of important philosophical problems. The complex and often strangely worded theories of philosophers are usually not likely to stimulate interest until one has seen how these theories are responses to legitimate philosophical problems, in which one has already become interested. After all, there is little point in presenting answers to questions that have not yet been asked. By understanding the problems that generated the theories, one becomes less prone to a general rejection of philosophy on the basis of a limited exposure to some bizarre-sounding theories.

Philosophers, as do other professionals, often write in a specialized language designed to facilitate the business of defending and evaluating competing theories. And the theories in question will often represent reactions to still other issues. But no matter how complex or involved philosophical theories may become, they are basically responses to problems ultimately linked to the familiar contexts of art, morality, science, religion, and common sense. At the edges of these familiar areas, philosophers discover latent problems; they do not simply invent them out of nothing. These familiar areas harbor the problems most likely to lure one into a general study of philosophy.

To illustrate some of the preceding points, let us see how nonphilosophers may be led into philosophical thinking, usually by way of an issue directly relevant to their special interests. Consider the following examples:

1. The neurophysiologist who, while establishing correlations between certain brain events and the feeling of pain, begins to wonder whether these correlations establish the *identity* of both types of events or a *causal* dependence of mental events on brain events — that is, whether the "mind" is distinct from the brain.

2. The nuclear physicist who, having determined that matter is mostly empty space containing colorless energy transformations, begins to wonder to what extent the solid, extended, colored world we perceive corresponds to what actually exists, and which world is the more "real."

3. The behavioral psychologist who, having increasing success in determining the specific causes of human behavior, questions whether any human actions can be called "free."

4. The Supreme Court justices who, faced with the task of distinguishing between obscene and nonobscene art forms for purposes of making law, are ultimately drawn into questions regarding the nature and function of art.

5. The theologian who, finding himself in a losing battle with science over literal descriptions of what the universe (or "reality") is actually like, is forced to redefine the whole purpose and scope of traditional theology.

6. The anthropologist who, noting that all societies have some conception of a moral code, begins to wonder just what distinguishes a moral from a nonmoral point of view.

7. The linguist who, in examining the various ways in which language shapes our view of the world, declares that there is no one "true reality" because all views of reality are conditioned and qualified by the language through which they must be expressed.

8. The perennial skeptic who, accustomed to demanding and not receiving absolute proof for every view he encounters, declares that it is impossible to know anything.

9. The concerned father who, having decided to convert his communist son, is forced to read Marx's original works and engage in some abstract reflection on the assumptions of Marxist versus capitalist ideology.

We could continue this list of examples indefinitely. These few should suffice, however, to point out that even for those individuals who have no native desire to pursue philosophical studies in general, there are often problems particularly relevant to their interests capable of luring them into a modest amount of philosophical thinking. The art critic probably could not care less about problems in the philosophy of science, yet the chances are that he could be led into a discussion concerning the nature of aesthetic experience. Thus, for the nonphilosopher who fails to see any "purpose" in the discipline, an effective response is to present him with philosophical problems of special relevance to his interests. In examining possible responses to those issues, he will discover that he is already tacitly committed to certain philosophical theses.

This completes our third, and final, response to the question "Why philosophize?" You may find some of the problems you encounter in your introductory course so interesting and worthy of further investigation, however, that this question will become less and less relevant. You will then find yourself on the inside of philosophy involved with philosophical issues rather than on the outside waiting to be convinced that you should participate.

Postscript: Are gurus philosophers?

As most of you know, gurus are spiritual masters who have purportedly achieved something ultimately real and inherently valuable — enlightenment and serenity. Through a variety of verbal and nonverbal techniques, for example, koans (riddles with no rational answers) and meditation in the case of Zen masters, they help others to achieve or approximate this state. Because of the profound and sometimes plausible ring of some of their claims, it is tempting to think of gurus as philosophers. There are, however, several important differences that undermine this classification.

Let us begin by considering the twin purposes of bringing enlightenment and serenity to those who seek them. In the first place, serenity is a *state of mind*, a condition of calmness or imperturbability relatively unaffected by the changing circumstances of the world. We recall, however, that the purpose of philosophy is not to induce any particular psychological state of being. Of course, anything from depression to ecstasy may *result* from one's encounter with philosophy. But achieving a certain state of mind is not a primary objective of doing philosophy. In this respect, then, the purposes of the philosopher and the guru do not overlap.

Perhaps, however, they overlap in the purpose of helping to enlighten interested persons. After all, philosophers do attempt to clarify, improve, and expand our understanding in certain respects. Although initially plausible, this coincidence of purpose must be qualified in several ways. First, for the guru, enlightenment tends to be viewed not only as an end in itself but also, and perhaps more importantly, as a *means* to the end of serenity. Consider the following passage: "Why are you unhappy? Because 99.9 percent of everything you think, and of everything you do, is for yourself — and there isn't one."[6] Enlightenment in this case would consist in giving up the illusion that we are distinct "selves" — in seeing that we are literally an integral part of nature. In so doing, according to this theory, we shall achieve at least a greater degree of happiness. For philosophers, however, rational enlightenment is not posed as a means to some further psychological state.

Second, many of the philosophical-sounding insights gurus express are closer to psychological generalizations about human nature. The following passage by a Zen master expresses the belief that happiness (the objective) is increased by avoiding pretense and role-playing: "Without any intentional, fancy way of adjusting yourself, to express yourself as you are is the most important thing."[7]

Third, gurus do express a relatively large number of philosophically interesting themes, more so than the average mathematician, politician, or housewife. To claim that truth is within oneself, that selfhood is an illusion, and that reality is in a continual process of change is to take a stand on philosophical issues. Unfortunately, however, merely asserting such theses, even if done regularly, does not make one a philosopher. To "join the club," one must *do* philosophy, a criterion that gurus generally fail to satisfy. For doing philosophy involves both developing and defending one's claim to truth on the basis of rational argumentation. And as a rule, gurus are not concerned with justifying rationally the truth of their insights. One does not debate a guru but rather requests clarification from him as an authority, someone who already has Truth. Indeed, many gurus are mildly amused by the conceptual difficulties with which philosophers struggle and point out that genuine enlightenment is not attainable merely by *thinking.*

There are, then, substantial differences between gurus and philosophers. Of course, these differences themselves imply nothing about the relative merits of belonging to one group in preference to the other. Rather, knowledge of these and other differences should be used merely to clarify and possibly reshape the expectations we have of both gurus and philosophers.

Notes

1. This is particularly true of some recent theologians who are less concerned with questions of existence or truth, such as "Is it true that Christ is God's earthly representative?" than with the relevance or "existential" significance of the Gospels for contemporary life. For example, the emphasis may be placed on applying Christian principles to personal and social problems rather than on believing in God. Compare, for example, Paul Tillich, *The Dynamics of Faith* (New York: Harper and Row, 1957); and Harvey Cox, *The Secular City* (New York: Macmillan, 1966).

2. The depiction of this tradition as "Socratic" is largely arbitrary, although its central themes are traceable to Socrates (479-399 B.C.) and to his student, Plato. With some notable exceptions, this tradition spans the history of Western philosophy. For a very useful and more detailed survey of the scope and influence of the Socratic (or what Passmore calls the "Platonic") view, consult John Passmore's article "Philosophy," in the *Encyclopedia of Philosophy*, Paul Edwards, ed. (New York: Macmillan, 1967). For a clear, though more narrowly conceived, defense by a contemporary philosopher working within that tradition, see Brand Blanshard's "In Defense of Metaphysics," in *Metaphysics: Readings and Reappraisals*, W. E. Kennick and M. Lazerowitz, eds. (Englewood Cliffs, N.J.: Prentice-Hall, 1961), p. 331.

3. Analytic philosophy is a twentieth-century movement, beginning with the writings of G. E. Moore and Bertrand Russell, and including such later philosophers as A. J. Ayer, Ludwig Wittgenstein, Gilbert Ryle, and John Austin. In one form or another, analytic philosophy is the dominant current trend in Anglo-American philosophy. Helpful surveys are found in Morris Weitz's article "Analysis," in the *Encyclopedia of Philosophy* (New York: Macmillan, 1967), and in his collection of readings, *Twentieth-Century Philosophy: The Analytic Tradition* (New York: Macmillan, 1966). Several good overviews of analytic philosophy are found in G. J. Warnock, *English Philosophy Since 1900* (New York: Oxford University Press, 1958); in selected chapters of John Passmore, *One Hundred Years of Philosophy*, 2nd ed. (New York: Basic Books, 1966); and in D. J. O'Connor, ed., *A Critical History of Western Philosophy* (New York: The Free Press, 1964).

4. Although this was generally true during the heyday of analytic philosophy, in recent years there has been a drift back to the Socratic

conception of philosophy's *purpose* while retaining a commitment to the *methods* of analytic philosophy.

5. The existential tradition begins in the nineteenth century with Sören Kierkegaard and Friedrich Nietzsche, and includes in this century Martin Heidegger, Jean-Paul Sartre, Gabriel Marcel, and Karl Jaspers. In the twentieth century, existentialism is closely related to a distinctive view of philosophical method called *phenomenology* (the science of pure description). In different forms, these schools represent the dominant trend on the European continent. A good collection of representative readings is: Robert C. Solomon, ed., *Existentialism* (New York: Modern Library, 1974). A short survey of existentialist themes is found in Alasdair MacIntyre's article, "Existentialism," in the *Encyclopedia of Philosophy* (New York: Macmillan, 1967). For a longer discussion, consult Robert G. Olson, *An Introduction to Existentialism* (New York: Dover, 1962). A delightful, though less accessible, overview with particular reference to contemporary literature is Gordon Bigelow's "A Primer of Existentialism," *College English*, December, 1961.

6. Wei Wu Wei, *Ask the Awakened*, (London: Routledge and Kegan Paul, 1963), p. xxi.

7. Shunryu Suzuki, *Zen Mind, Beginner's Mind* (New York: John Weatherhill, 1970), p. 82.

Chapter III

Doing Philosophy

Since philosophers do not rely on scientific method, they must depend instead on different forms of rational investigation and evaluation. Our purpose in this chapter is to examine some basic critical tools philosophers use, so that you will have the means to tackle the issues raised in your first course in philosophy.[1] You may be surprised to learn that many of these techniques are no different in principle from those one might expect to find in other disciplines. What makes certain arguments "philosophical" often stems more from the subject matter than from some esoteric reasoning process to which only philosophers have access.

Preparing to philosophize.

Before undertaking our survey, several preliminary matters require attention. First, philosophizing, insofar as it involves you in discussion with fellow students and with your instructor, is but one form of communication. As such, it involves certain psychological traits that should be encouraged in the interest of communicating effectively. It requires: (1) the courage to put one's cherished beliefs on the line for critical scrutiny; (2) a willingness to advance tentative hypotheses and to take the first step in reacting to a philosophical claim, no matter how foolish your reaction might seem at the time; (3) a desire to place the search for truth above the satisfaction of apparently "winning" the debate or the frustration of "losing" it; (4) an ability to separate matters of personality from the content of a discussion. A failure to make this separation may result in cloudy thinking and a conflict of personalities that can subvert the possibility of progress.

Second, responsible philosophizing is a *skill* that must be developed with practice. It is more akin to the abilities of a competent surgeon or race-car driver than to those of a computer programmer. There are few "cookbook" rules in philosophy that can be simply memorized and universally applied to all problems with much assurance that an adequate answer will result. This lack of prescribed rules is largely due to the extremely diverse and fluid nature of philosophical subject matter. Just as the race-car driver must apply his prior general knowledge of mechanics, aerodynamics, and the like to shifting conditions during a particular race, the methods we shall examine must be applied sensitively, with an awareness of the peculiarities of the specific issue.

Third, *doing* philosophy rather than just *studying* it is intellectually challenging. Many of you may have come to your first course with the tacit assumption that theoretical problems are to be resolved in one of two ways. The first is by appeal to authority, whether in the form of a professor, a textbook of facts, or an application of scientific method. If these methods are unavailable, then any proposed resolution, you may be tempted to conclude, must boil down to a matter of personal preference.

Unfortunately, these two approaches are neither fruitful nor correct in philosophy. For one reason, the "authorities" are themselves continually undergoing critical examination in an effort to sift the enduring truth of their views from those parts that cannot withstand criticism. In addition, personal attitudes provide at best a point of departure for criticizing a certain view, not a standard for evaluating competing arguments. "I like this view" is never a good reason in philosophy. The question is rather "*Why* do you think this is the best position?" The alternative to the extremes of appealing to authority or deciding an issue by personal preference is to exercise one's own reason critically — informed, of course, by knowledge of the facts of the issue. It is difficult to do this while avoiding the extremes of exclusive reliance on either authority or undisciplined personal bias.

Fourth, fruitful philosophizing is not to be confused with doing psychology, in particular with the tendency to explain persons' (philosophical) beliefs by reference to the *causes* — for example, childhood training, social pressure, other psychological motives — that may have prompted those beliefs. (The attempt to justify or criticize a certain belief rationally merely by determining its causal origins is called the "genetic fallacy.") Philosophers look rather for the *reasons* that might be cited for or against, say, the view that God exists. The 'why' in "Why does Jones believe in God?" in a philosophy class thus should not be answered with "Because Jones was conditioned by his parents and his Sunday school lessons to believe in God" or "Because Jones is insecure and feels better with the idea of a father-figure." To take a different example, it is a task for psychology to discover the causes of persons' commitments to certain political ideologies, a task for philosophy to isolate the theoretical justifications and criticisms of those ideologies.

Fifth, philosophy has two sides, one critical, the other constructive. It is one task, for example, to criticize John Locke's social-contract theory of government, quite another to improve on it! The methods we shall survey, however, favor the critical aspect. Two closely related facts suggest slanting the discussion in this direction. To begin with, learning to analyze a position critically is generally necessary for doing good theoretical speculation. In this way, undetected mistakes in developing one's own philosophy will more likely be avoided. Also, in exposing the weaknesses of other theories, the lines along which a new theory should be developed often emerge naturally. Of course, there is no substitute for creative insight. Avoiding the criticisms levelled at other theories will often take one a good distance down the road toward the view to which he will ultimately subscribe. With these preliminary observations in mind, then, let us begin a survey of some basic critical tools.

What type of claim is advanced?

Different types of claims are evaluated by different criteria. For example, we do not judge a work of art in the same way that we do a scientific hypothesis. Hence, before we can evaluate the correctness or adequacy of a statement, we need to know what type of claim is being advanced. To distinguish claims of philosophical interest from those that are not philosophically significant is one of the philosopher's first jobs. The matter is often not this simple, however. A single sentence may embody several types of claims, in which case the job is again one of isolating those that are philosophically significant from those that are not. For this latter job, the criteria discussed in Chapter I are relevant. Consider the following examples:

1. All children in Zululand receive moral training.
2. Moral acts are never performed for altruistic motives.
3. A moral person is one who follows his conscience.
4. Abortion is not moral.
5. To be morally responsible for an act, it must have been performed freely.
6. No moral person does what he thinks is right.

Each of these claims involves the concept of morality. But they employ it in different and overlapping ways. Let us see how.

The first sentence is a straightforward empirical claim, the truth or falsity of which the philosopher is not concerned to evaluate. That would be a job for the sociologist or anthropologist.

On the surface, the second sentence looks like an empirical claim about the nature of human motivation and its causal relation to moral action. Its point is that all actions are actually performed for motives of self-interest. As a matter of empirical fact, it is claimed, persons are incapable of putting the interests of others ahead of their own. Certainly, there is some support for this thesis; we have all known individuals who did their duty or helped their fellowman simply to enhance their own interests. But empirical claims, we recall, must admit of some potential counterevidence. That is, they must be falsifiable in principle. And this claim, as it is usually advanced in a universal or absolute form, is made immune to counterevidence. If the claim is questioned on empirical grounds — for example, by citing the fact that Jones, Smith, and Wilson put the educational interests of their children ahead of their own by moonlighting, an opponent could respond that they were really just looking out after their own prestige or future interests. Perhaps they want to be well taken care of in their old age. It usually doesn't take many such examples to see that the claim is made true largely by arbitrary decree, not by careful empirical investigation.

The third sentence is partly or wholly definitional. It says in effect that at least one defining feature (there may be more) of any moral person is that he acts consistently with the dictates of his conscience. So, what we need here are some criteria for evaluating definitions. These criteria will be considered shortly, at which point we will see that both empirical and logical considerations play a role.

The fourth sentence is neither empirical nor definitional. Rather, the claim it embodies is a moral judgment to the effect that no abortion satisfies certain standards which a morally right action must satisfy. Already, several different courses of analysis are opened up, indeed required, to evaluate this claim. What are those moral standards? Are they adequate? (*Adequacy* also will be discussed shortly.) How applicable are they to abortions?

The fifth sentence is unlike any of its predecessors, although it assumes certain definitions of 'moral', 'responsible', and 'freedom'. This claim asserts a logical connection between 'freedom' and 'responsibility'. Freedom of action is a necessary condition of ascribing moral responsibility.

The sixth sentence is necessarily, not contingently, false. Jones's conception of right actions may indeed be quite different from one's own. But 'moral' is always used in such a way as to entail that the agent does what *he* believes to be right. The sentence violates the limits of that usage. It thus expresses a conceptual impossibility.

What is the meaning of key concepts?

Clarifying meaning is one of the philosopher's most important activities. Before one can evaluate the correctness or adequacy of a philosophical thesis, one must understand the thesis he is evaluating. It is impossible to determine the truth or falsity of a claim such as "Machines cannot be conscious," for example, until one ascertains just what is involved in anything's being conscious. In this section, we shall examine two of the most important methods of clarifying meaning — (1) presenting paradigm and borderline examples and (2) developing adequate definitions.

First, the use of *paradigm* examples plays a strategic role in clarifying meaning. Paradigm examples illustrate the core meaning of concepts. Martin Luther King is a paradigm of the concept of a nonviolent, black civil-rights leader, just as Albert Einstein is a paradigm of scientific genius, Christianity of religion, the *Mona Lisa* of great art, and Hitler's extermination of six million Jews of moral atrocity. For any concept, there are usually a number of potential paradigms.

Paradigm cases often function as a point of departure for clarifying concepts. When asked to define 'justice' or 'intelligence', for example, many of us may be struck temporarily speechless. Rather than attempting to present an adequate definition immediately, a helpful strategy is to cite a paradigm case and then to identify the particular properties of that case which seem to justify its being an instance of the concept in question. For example, what is a moral prophet? Well, Jesus was such a prophet. What essential characteristics of Jesus suggest this classification? Perhaps one characteristic is his articulation of an effective and novel set of principles for guiding interpersonal relations — for example, love thy neighbor; turn the other cheek; and judge not lest you be judged. This characteristic, then, should be incorporated into the definition of 'moral prophet'.

Paradigms function as anchoring points from which definitions can eventually be built; they help to insure adequacy. The paradigm's implicit form is: "If case X is not an instance of concept Y, then I don't know what is!" An example might be: "I don't know what your concept of pornography is, but it must at least include photographs of the public exhibition of sexual intercourse."

Using *borderline*, or limiting, examples is often helpful when, although we may understand clearly the essential meaning of certain concepts, we are not certain how far that meaning extends. Borderline examples help to clarify the limits of a given concept's applicability. For instance, is Confucianism a religion? That is, does 'religion' apply to Confucianism? Some commentators have noted that Confucianism is almost exclusively concerned with social relations — for example, reverence for authority, the family, and so on — and have concluded that it should not be classified as a religion. Confucianism seems to lack what other religions, such as Christianity and Judaism, have, namely, a conception of a divine being and humankind's relation to this being. Thus Confucianism falls outside the limits of religion. Of course, one may argue that Confucianism should be classified as a religion precisely because of its emphasis upon social relations and the proper conduct of life, irrespective of the incorporation of a concept of a divine being. Whichever way we decide, however, certain limits of applicability of 'religion' will be correspondingly clarified, and the meaning of that concept will be understood to extend to those limits.

Borderline examples must sometimes be invented when no actual cases readily appear. Suppose that a strange drug were released into the earth's atmosphere, having the effect that things once perceived as green are now perceived as red. Does this entail that those same objects are now in reality red? What would the answer to this question tell us about our concepts of color and perception? Could we infer that if enough persons agree about what they see, they are in possession of perceptual knowledge? Or, suppose the change were gradual. Would there come a point when we could no longer say we knew whether those objects were green or red? The purpose of raising such hypothetical possibilities is not merely to stimulate the imagination but also to exercise our intellects in the clarification of meaning.

Let us now examine a second method of clarifying meaning, that of developing adequate *definitions*. How does one determine whether a proposed definition is adequate? The answer to this question depends largely on first determining the type of definition proposed. Although there are many different types of definitions, we shall focus attention on two in particular — (1) reportive and (2) reformative.

A *reportive* definition states the meaning(s) of a concept as it is used in our language.[2] It reports what is generally understood to be the meaning of the particular concept. A reportive definition of 'automobile', for example, would be "four-wheeled, motorized vehicle designed for the transportation of a few people over land." Dictionary entries are usually reportive. A definition may be reportive even if it expresses a technical or specialized sense commonly understood only by the members of some particular group. Within the community of physicists, for example, 'neutrino' has an established common meaning that admits of a reportive definition. Linguistic usage provides a reasonably objective standard by which the correctness of a reportive definition may be tested. To define 'tobacco' as "any substance that may be smoked," for example, is simply wrong. 'Tobacco' is not used in this way.

In providing a definition, one states the essential characteristics that something must possess in order to be referred to by the concept being defined. For example, the properties of being male and unmarried must be possessed by any person who qualifies as a bachelor. These properties must accordingly be incorporated into a definition of 'bachelor'. In stating the essential characteristics, one establishes limits regarding what falls within the scope of the concept being defined. How these limits are determined distinguishes among the various types of definitions.

In the case of reportive definitions, limits are determined by insuring that the concept and its reported meaning both fit the same cases. If they do not, then the proposed definition will have to be changed. For example, if "one who attends church regularly" were an adequate definition of 'moral person', then all persons whom we describe as moral would be churchgoers *and* all churchgoers would be describable as moral. As a matter of fact, this is not the case; there are both immoral churchgoers and moral nonchurchgoers.

These facts suggest a very simple technique for evaluating the correctness of reportive definitions — the method of counterexample. A counterexample is a fact that allegedly falsifies a certain claim, in this case, a definition. Consider the claim that 'love' means "emotional involvement." Are there any persons whom we would say are in love yet not emotionally attached in some way? Probably not. There do not appear to be any counterexamples to the thesis that if a person is in love, then he or she is also emotionally attached. All persons in love fall within the class of those emotionally attached in some way. Counterexamples, however, work both ways in evaluating reportive definitions. Simply by virtue of their emotional attachment, some persons do not necessarily love the object of their emotion. One individual may be emotionally dependent on another, for instance, yet be totally insensitive to his or her needs and lack all respect for the other. It is possible, therefore, to discover a counterexample to the thesis that if a person is emotionally attached, then he or she is in love. "Being in love" and "being emotionally attached" do not apply to the same range of persons. The conceptual limits in question do not coincide; rather, one concept "contains" the other. This is illustrated in the following diagram.

'Love' ← means? → "emotionally involved"

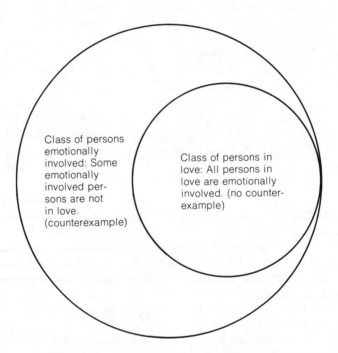

In an adequate definition there would be
no counterexamples and the two circles
would coincide.

The use of counterexamples is reasonably objective insofar as it is based on empirical facts. Indeed, this is one of the most common ways empirical data may figure in philosophical investigation. Whether defensible or not, 'love' is taken to mean more than "emotional involvement." The formulation of a reportive definition and the determination of its limits must remain true to those facts — as every dictionary editor knows. When we come to _reformative_ definitions, however, we will see that the picture changes considerably.

Although they are not always successful, reformative definitions are intended to be better explications of the meaning of the concept in question. Their proponents are less concerned with commonly subscribed to meanings than with the truth of the matter. One is being prepared for a reformative definition when someone announces: "I'm going to tell you what love _really_ is!" Reformative definitions constitute profound and interesting, yet troublesome, proposals in philosophy. How should they be evaluated? Although reformative definitions can be arbitrary (a possibility to be discussed shortly), they usually are not in philosophy. Often they conform partially to common meanings with which we are already familiar. To this extent, they may be evaluated along the empirical lines just described in the previous example. The newer, more provocative, aspect of the definition that allegedly captures the truth of the matter, however, must be examined in relation to the _reasons_ that are advanced on its behalf. The task becomes one of analyzing the arguments that a philosopher proposes for changing the meaning of a certain concept, or perhaps even introducing an entirely new concept. Let us note briefly how such changes may be set forth.

A nearly total change in the meaning of a familiar concept is found in the philosopher Leibniz's (1646-1716) criticism of the concept of an atom. Leibniz argued that the prevailing definition of an 'atom' as "the simplest unit of matter" was inherently self-contradictory. His argument was that, since whatever is material must have dimension, and whatever has dimension can always be further divided, no unit of matter can ever be the simplest. The expression "simplest unit of matter" thus mistakenly conjoins two concepts in a way precluded by their meaning. Leibniz concluded that, in order to escape contradiction, we must conceive of the simplest units of which things are composed as _immaterial._ He labeled these immaterial units 'monads'.

First, what is arbitrary about this proposal for a shift in meaning is Leibniz's decision to introduce the word 'monad'. He might have retained the term 'atom', were it not for the fact that whenever one proposes a drastic change in meaning of a familiar concept, it is desirable to coin a new term to avoid confusion. Second, Leibniz did retain part of the common meaning of 'atom', namely, the notion of a simple, distinct entity of which things are composed. Third, and most important, his proposal to change the remaining part of the original meaning from "material" to "immaterial" was supported by an argument. And the way we evaluate this proposal is neither by appealing to an "I-don't-choose-to-define-it-that-way" attitude nor by insisting that the original definition is, after all, the "real" definition, since that definition is precisely what is called into question. Rather, we must *evaluate the arguments* Leibniz (or any philosopher) advances for changing — that is, *reforming* — the meaning of the concept in question.

One mistake to avoid is that of making a theory true by definition. In practice, this often amounts to asserting a definition that appears at first to be reportive but turns out to be arbitrary. Consider the claim that a religious person is one who believes in a supreme being of some sort. Now, this is certainly not a complete definition of what it means to be religious. Many would insist that certain *actions* must also accompany this belief. Nevertheless, it is partially correct as a reportive definition. Persons do use 'religious' to entail "believes in a supreme being."

Suppose someone points out, however, that some religions do not necessarily involve this belief, for example, Hinayana Buddhism. This amounts to a denial that belief in a supreme being is a necessary condition of being religious. The shift from a reportive to a partly arbitrary definition occurs if the proponent still insists that such belief is essential to religion. He is then forced into holding that Hinayana Buddhists are not really religious because their beliefs are not consistent with *his* definition of religion. In effect, he will not permit exceptions to his definition. The difficulty with this and all such approaches is that any thesis can be made true by definition. The Buddhist could just as easily claim that any person who does believe in a supreme being is not really religious. A definition that is both made immune to counterexamples and is not rationally supportable is arbitrary. And arbitrary definitions in philosophy should always be avoided.

Are the supporting arguments valid?

Before discussing validity, we need to touch briefly on the subject of recognizing arguments. *Arguments* are composed entirely of statements, one of which (the conclusion) allegedly follows from, or is supported by, the others (premises). Statements may be defined as true or false sentences. Unfortunately, many philosophical and nonphilosophical arguments are not initially set forth in a clear, one-two-three fashion. The conclusion, for example, may be both preceded and followed by supporting premises in a relatively jumbled manner; the conclusion is not always presented at the end of an argument. To distinguish between the premises and conclusion, it is helpful to keep in mind that expressions such as 'since', 'because', and 'in view of the facts that' usually introduce premises, and expressions such as 'hence', 'therefore', and 'it follows that' usually introduce the conclusion.

The appearance of one of these expressions, however, does not necessarily imply that what follows is a premise or a conclusion. For example, the sentence "Since you didn't heed my warning, I therefore order you to cease" does not express an argument at all. Why not? To begin with, the second clause, which perhaps looks like a conclusion, is not a *statement* about what is the case but rather is a command. (Commands may be just or unjust, but they cannot be true or false.) And arguments, you will recall, are composed entirely of statements, not commands, questions, or exclamations. In addition, the first clause, which perhaps looks like a premise, does not express evidence for the truth of some other claim. Instead, it expresses a brief explanation of why the command is being given.

Once you have ascertained that an argument is advanced and have distinguished between the premises and conclusion, it is often helpful to abstract the relevant statements from their context — perhaps rewrite them more clearly and concisely — and arrange them such that the premises precede the conclusion. As an example, the following passage expresses an argument that is rewritten in its proper form directly beneath it: "I cannot be identical with my body, since I can doubt whether my body exists, but I cannot doubt that I exist, and if they were the same they should be equally dubitable."

1. If I am identical with my body, then my existence and my body's existence should be equally dubitable.
2. I cannot doubt that I exist.
3. I can doubt that my body exists.
4. Hence, my existence and my body's existence are not equally dubitable.
5. Therefore, I am not identical with my body.

Now, how do we determine the validity of an argument? Validity is one of the criteria with which we evaluate deductive, as opposed to inductive, arguments. A *deductive* argument is one in which it is claimed that the conclusion is necessarily implied by the premises. The above argument, for example, is deductive. If a deductive argument is valid, there exists a *necessary* link between the premises and conclusion. An *inductive* argument, in contrast, is one in which it is claimed that if the premises are true, they bestow a certain degree of probability on the conclusion. A simple example is: "Heart trouble occurs more frequently among smokers than among nonsmokers, so smoking is (probably) instrumental in bringing on heart trouble." No matter how true or complete the evidence expressed by the premises, there always exists a *contingent* link between the premises and the conclusion of an inductive argument.

Validity concerns the structure or form of a deductive argument, not the truth or falsity of the individual premises and conclusion. One way to determine the validity of a supporting argument, therefore, is to see whether it possesses a valid argument form. Some common forms together with their appropriate names are:

Modus Ponens	Modus Tollens	Hypothetical Syllogism	Disjunctive Syllogism
If p then q	If p then q	If p then q	Either p or q
p	Not q	If q then r	Not p
Therefore, q	Hence, not p	Hence, if p then r	Therefore, q

In each of these argument forms, P, Q, and R are arbitrarily chosen letters that stand for simple sentences. No matter what we substitute for p, q, or r, the resulting argument will be valid. For instance, in the first form, *modus ponens*, we might substitute "fetuses are human" for p and "abortion is murder" for q. The result would be:

1. If fetuses are human (p), then abortion is murder (q).
2. Fetuses are human (p).
3. Therefore, abortion is murder (q).

The premises and conclusion may be false (that is a different problem), but the argument is valid.

A different kind of deductive reasoning consists in drawing inferences based on *class membership* rather than on relations between simple sentences, as the above forms illustrate. Class membership may be affirmed (partly or wholly) or denied (partly or wholly). These possibilities may be combined to give us a relatively large number of argument forms. A few are:

All p is s	No s is p	All p is r	Some s is not r
No r is s	Some r is p	Jones is p	All p is r
No r is p	Some r is not s	Jones is r	Some s is not p

In these argument forms, p, r, and s denote classes of things, such as persons with red hair, democrats, true believers, toads, or revolutionaries — whatever classes happen to be in question. For example, if p, r, and s stand for true believers, democrats, and revolutionaries, respectively, then we may construct the following valid argument:

1. All true believers (p) are revolutionaries (s).
2. No democrats (r) are revolutionaries (s).
3. Therefore, no democrats (r) are true believers (p).

Again, you may question the truth of the individual statements, but the inference is valid.

There are literally hundreds of valid as well as invalid argument forms which, short of presenting a course in logic, we cannot begin to survey. However, a general rule of thumb will enable you to test a deductive argument for its validity without having to rely on the sort of formal proof procedures you would learn in a logic course. This rule, which is based on the definition of validity, involves the use of counterexamples. A valid argument is one such that *if* the premises are true, then the conclusion must also be true. Alternatively, if the argument is valid, it cannot possess all true premises and a false conclusion. So, if one can conceive of circumstances under which the premises would be true and the conclusion would be false, then one will have proved the argument in question invalid. Consider the following example:

1. If you study, you'll pass the final.
2. But you can't study.
3. So you won't pass the final.

It is possible that both of the premises are true here, yet you nevertheless pass the final, perhaps by cheating or guessing, in which case the original conclusion will have been rendered false. Now, you may *happen* to fail the exam. But in the present deductive argument, the claim is that *if* the premises are true and the inference valid, you *must* fail the exam. If it is even *possible* that the premises are all true and the conclusion false, then the argument is invalid.

Are the premises true?

To be sound, a deductive argument must possess both a valid form of inference *and* true premises. If either is missing, the argument is unsound and should be rejected. We have just seen how to test the validity of a deductive argument. The difficulty with determining the truth of the premises is that all philosophical arguments contain at least one nonempirical premise (sometimes more), the truth of which cannot be determined simply by an appeal to experience, scientific authority, or the dictionary. Most of your efforts directed toward determining the truth of the premises in general will therefore be focused on the nonempirical premises in particular. There are, you will recall, different types of nonempirical assertions, corresponding to which are certain methods of evaluation appropriate to the type of claim in question. For example, if the premise asserts a logical connection between two or more concepts, then additional methods are appropriate for its evaluation. Let us discuss some of these additional methods.

Are the assumptions correct?

A philosophical thesis may have assumptions in either or both of two senses. First, an assumption may function as a *necessary* condition of a certain theory; second, an assumption may function as a *sufficient* condition of that theory. The particular sense in which the assumption is used largely determines the logical effectiveness of questioning its correctness. We shall examine both senses and make clear their relevance for critical strategy.

When an assumption (or several assumptions taken collectively) is a sufficient condition for a certain theory, then we say that it (they) *entails* that theory. That is, given the assumption, the theory follows; if the assumption is true, then so is the theory. For example, holding an orthodox Marxist economic theory is a sufficient condition of rejecting as false the central tenets of laissez-faire capitalism — for example, that market prices should be determined by the free interaction of supply and demand.

Someone who attacks this tenet may be led to do so because, unknown to you, he already assumes the truth of orthodox Marxism. Then again, he might not assume its truth. There are several reasons one may advance in criticizing the thesis of free-market price determination, independent of Marxian assumptions. One does not have to be a Marxist to criticize capitalism.

The practical significance of this fact is that even if Marxist economic theory is wrong, the free-market thesis may still be correct *or* it may also be indefensible. Thus, if you wish to defend that thesis, showing the mistakes of the Marxian assumptions that perhaps led your adversary to attack the thesis will not be decisive, although it would be partially effective. The same is true for all assumptions that function as sufficient conditions of theories you may wish to question.

A more powerful and direct strategy is to attack those assumptions that are necessary conditions of the theory in question. Such assumptions are called *presuppositions*. Necessary conditions of a view must be correct in order for the view itself to be correct; their truth is a condition of the truth of that view. In other words, necessary conditions are entailed by the theory for which they are the presuppositions. Thus, to show their falsehood is to undermine directly the view you wish to reject.

In questioning the necessary assumptions of a theory, it is often helpful to use the *modus tollens* form of argumentation described earlier. This form begins with a hypothetical premise (If *p* then *q*). The logical relation of a theory to one of its necessary assumptions is expressed by that premise. The rejection of the assumption is expressed by the second premise (not *q*). And your rejection of the theory is given in the conclusion (not *p*). Suppose, for example, that you decide to examine the thesis "Persons survive the death of their bodies" by questioning the assumption(s) on which it is based. One such assumption is that our thoughts, memories, and feelings are now numerically distinct from our bodies and brains. (Otherwise, what would be "left over" when our bodies die?) Your overall strategy might take the following form:

1. If persons survive the death of their bodies, then our thoughts, memories, experiences, and so forth must now be distinct from our bodies and brains.
2. But thoughts, memories, experiences, and so forth are identical with certain states of our brains, and are therefore not distinct from them.
3. Therefore, persons do not survive the death of their bodies (brains).

Of course, for this to be a sound argument (true premises plus a valid inference), the second premise in particular must be supported with reasons, since it is the second premise that your philosophical adversary is most likely to reject. The above format merely illustrates an overall strategy in examining a thesis through its assumptions.

Clearly, not all assumptions fit neatly into the dichotomy of necessary or sufficient conditions. There are always borderline cases. Often, assumptions are hidden in the background, that is, are unconsciously held, and must be brought to the surface by critical dialogue. Indeed, critical discussion is often the only means of determining the exact role that certain assumptions may play in a theory. Suppose, for example, that someone asserts that ceasing to require a morning recitation of the Lord's Prayer in public schools is an attack on religion. Three possible assumptions of this claim are: (1) that 'religion' means "Christianity", to which the Lord's Prayer is uniquely tied; (2) that being religious means believing in a superior being; (3) that religious education is best served by public communal expressions of prayer. Now (1) and (2) probably represent necessary conditions, whereas (3) probably comes close to being a sufficient condition of the thesis — at least in the mind of its proponent. In the absence of further clarification, the issue is certainly debatable. However, no matter what the assumptions of a theory may be or what their exact role is, showing their incorrectness will generally undermine that theory and/or its sources of support. Questioning assumptions is always a sound critical strategy.

Evaluating assumptions is one of the primary tasks of philosophy. This is not only because we wish to avoid committing ourselves to mistaken or inadequate views but also because a knowledge of *shared* assumptions is often essential to making positive advances in philosophical discussion. All of us bring to our respective judgments certain implicit principles and ideals. These assumptions provide a standard by which those judgments may be evaluated. We judge according to our ideological commitments, whether they be to Christianity, conservatism, humanism, or astrology. For example, two Christians who assume that the Bible is the revealed word of God may use that belief as a standard to help decide the issue of whether salvation is attainable through good works alone. They may not ultimately agree, but at least the possibility of agreement is enhanced by the fact that they can rely on a common standard. The possibility of agreement is more remote in the case of someone who rejects the assumption that the Bible is the only revealed word of God. For example, how might a

Christian attempt to "save" a Buddhist? If his whole case is based on citing the Scriptures, his chances are lessened. If the Buddhist and the Christian are really to have a meaningful dialogue, they must first isolate certain common assumptions, such as the belief that religious commitment should lead to greater happiness and peace of mind. Similarly, in philosophy, determining common assumptions is an important prerequisite of progress.

Are the consequences plausible?

Another way to evaluate a theory consists in determining whether it has certain consequences that are themselves open to objection. If the consequences are objectionable, then the original thesis is objectionable. When certain consequences are shown to result from a thesis, that thesis is said to be a *sufficient* condition for their existence.

The *modus tollens* form of argument again provides a convenient logical framework within which to determine any undesirable consequences of a theory. Suppose that someone asserted the thesis mentioned earlier, that whatever exists must be observable. Your response would take the form: "If this claim is correct, then what follows?" One consequence might be that consciousness must then not exist, since it is unobservable. We might stop here with the conclusion that since consciousness obviously does exist, then there must be something wrong with the initial thesis. However, since 'consciousness' in the abstract gives persons conceptual difficulty sometimes, we could draw out a further, more concrete, consequence such as: "If consciousness does not exist, it follows that nobody is conscious, and (going still further) if nobody is conscious, then I must not be conscious as I think about this thesis. But this consequence is absurd; hence, there must be something wrong with the thesis."[3]

The most unacceptable consequence of a theory is one that renders the theory self-defeating. A theory is self-defeating if it logically involves two or more claims that are inconsistent with each other. For example, some philosophers, called Indeterminists, defined a free action as an *un*caused event, because they believed that if all events were caused, there could be no free acts and thus no moral responsibility — which they did want to preserve. The assumption of holding a person responsible, however, is that he or she (freely) caused or in some way brought about the act in question. Yet if the action was freely performed, it cannot have been caused. So, a consequence of this Indeterminist definition of a free act is that persons cannot be held responsible for their actions. And this is inconsistent with a central tenet of Indeterminism, namely, that persons can be held responsible for their acts. Hence, the above definition of freedom is self-defeating; one cannot consistently deny what he implicitly assumes — a fallacy that you should guard against in philosophical discussion.

How adequate is the theory?

The adequacy of a philosophical theory depends on how well it fits the data to be interpreted.[4] The "tightness of the fit" is determined by discovering potential counterexamples. If you can find examples that fit the theory, although they should not, or that do not fit the theory, although they should, then the adequacy of the theory is lessened. The process is similar to that used in evaluating reportive definitions.

Let's first consider the strategy of citing examples that fit the theory, but should not. At the end of the first chapter, we inferred from the claims that (1) 'good' means "whatever is natural," and that (2) sex is natural, that sex must therefore be good. But are all natural things "good" things? When we look at this principle itself, it is inadequate because it justifies too much. Among other things, it entails that terminal cancer must also be good because it, too, is natural. Again, few persons would want to hold that San Francisco's being swallowed by an earthquake is good. Citing this counterexample thus forces one to restrict, or qualify, his central principle. Natural objects or events are good so long as nobody is hurt by them. This qualification helps, but the principle still needs further restriction. Sticks and mud, for example, are natural and in themselves hurt nobody. Yet it is not at all clear that we would call them "good," too.

The alternative strategy — that of citing examples that should fit the theory if it is adequate, although they do not — is encountered frequently in philosophical evaluation. Classical materialists, for example, claimed that (with the exception of space and time) everything that exists is nothing more than variations of matter and motion. The difference between rocks and trees, they held, was basically a difference of the motion and position of atoms comprising those objects. This may sound good at first. But a comprehensive theory of existence must account for everything that in fact exists — if it claims to be adequate. It is hard to see how such things as electromagnetic energy, mental depression, and political values can be made to fit the categories of matter and motion. We observe the position of matter in space, for instance, but what sense would it make to measure the spatial position of a set of values? Again, mental depressions change, but do they move like material objects? The theory that reality is reducible to the categories of matter and motion needs to be expanded to cover the kinds of existence we ascribe to the counterexamples cited above.

Defects of adequacy are most common in attempts to develop a philosophical theory by generalizing from a very narrow base, particularly when the base happens to be one's own experience. Such defects of adequacy can be at least partly avoided by distinguishing between relatively universal experiences, for example, the feeling of pain, and experiences restricted to a smaller range of persons, for example, the feeling of leading a meaningless life. If, in the latter case, one generalizes from his personal feeling to the thesis that life is meaningless, he faces numerous counterexamples. Life just does not seem that way to many persons. Similar restrictions apply to the even more unique claim, "The mind must be distinct from the body because I've left my body on several occasions." Not only have the great majority of persons not had a similar experience, those who have would not necessarily interpret it as a case of actually leaving one's body. Generalizations based on personal experience should therefore be formulated with caution.

You will sometimes encounter philosophical theories asserting that what some persons believe to be instances of a certain category are really cases of another category. With such theories, the method of citing individual counterexamples is not usually effective, since all counterexamples will have been ruled out in advance. (Citing counterexamples in such cases may beg the issue, a logical fallacy we shall discuss in the following section.) Hence, a different strategy is required. For example, we claim to know what we directly observe ("I know he hit the dog because I saw him do it"). A few philosophers (skeptics), however, have argued that observation does not give us absolutely certain knowledge. For many persons, the skeptic's theory is inadequate. (If we do not know what we see, then what can we know?) Still, citing counterexamples based on sensory experience will usually be met with the skeptic's rejoinder that, after all, one *could* be mistaken about what he believes he sees, and genuine knowledge cannot admit of such a possibility. What one claims to "know" based on observation, therefore, will be rejected as not really being a counterexample. Thus, the inadequacy of the skeptic's view must be shown by attacking the arguments used to support it rather than by citing counterexamples. The skeptic asserts, for instance, that certainty is a defining criterion of knowledge — that is, a necessary characteristic for classifying a belief as an instance of knowledge. But is this anything more than an assertion? Is this alleged logical link (between 'certainty' and 'knowledge') perhaps merely an arbitrary stipulation? What is meant by 'certainty' in this context? The strategy implied by such questions is to uncover faulty definitions and arguments *leading to* the inadequate thesis.

Is the issue begged?

An argument *begs the issue* when it assumes, often in a disguised form, the truth of the claim it is supposed to demonstrate. A very simple illustration of this fallacy is the argument that God exists because the Bible so affirms, and the Bible is correct because it is the revealed word of God. In the last premise, one needs to assume the existence of God to claim that the Bible is divinely inspired, and this is what the argument is supposed to demonstrate in the first place.

Question-begging arguments take a variety of forms which involve assuming the truth of a claim that is undermined by competing arguments. Disagreements over what is legal versus what is moral provide a good source of examples. Suppose that Smith leaks certain top-secret documents to the press for the reason that, in this particular case, it would be in the best interests of the country for the public to know what its government is doing. Jones, however, claims that Smith should be punished because he broke the law. Smith then admits to breaking the law, but points out that his doing so is justified in the name of a "higher moral law," and that he should therefore not be punished. Unmoved, Jones insists that the law must be obeyed, to which Smith responds that his action is a legitimate exception. Is it? The debate between Smith and Jones appears to be deadlocked in a situation of mutual question-begging. Each bases his case on a principle that the other claims is not applicable in this situation. The issue of whether Smith should be punished is potentially begged, for instance, when Jones simply reaffirms his belief that law-breakers should be punished, after the applicability of this claim has been undermined by Smith's argument.

Understanding how to employ internal and external

criticisms can be useful in determining whether supporting arguments beg the issue. Briefly, an *internal* criticism attempts to show certain inherent difficulties in a thesis on grounds that are independent of the critic's own competing view. These difficulties may involve invalid arguments, unclear meaning, arbitrary assumptions, or consequences stranger than the proponent of the thesis ever imagined. Basically, the aim of an internal criticism is to enter momentarily into the proponent's point of view and to try to "beat him at his own game" using rules you both accept. For example, an internal objection to the thesis that the pursuit of pleasure is the best "philosophy of life" might be to show that, in various ways, too much pleasure can lead to undesirable consequences.

An *external* criticism, in contrast, is based on assumptions and "rules of the game" that are alien to, or inconsistent with, the central themes of the view under examination. Moreover, an external criticism is usually an integral part of the critic's own competing thesis. An external criticism of the preceding "philosophy of pleasure" is that it is simply false, because there are obviously many worthwhile goals and activities in life other than the pursuit of pleasure, for example, building character through hard work or attaining peace of mind through meditation.

The relevance of this internal-external distinction is that one stands a greater chance of begging crucial issues to the extent that he raises external criticisms of a theory, and less of a chance to the extent that he raises internal objections. For example, the scientist who rejects belief in God on the grounds that it involves claims that cannot be verified by applying scientific method (an external criticism) potentially begs the issue. It might be argued that God can be known either by direct mystical experience or that His existence can be proved by the exercise of pure reason, both of which means fall outside the scope of scientific methodology. What independent proof can the scientist offer that his methods are the only way to truth? More effective (internal) objections would be found in attempts to show that the concept of 'God' is meaningless or that He is not worthy of worship because He created a world full of evil. Camus — god is unjust

This concludes our overview of a few elementary techniques of evaluation that you should find useful in your encounter with philosophical problems. As we noted at the outset of the discussion, skill in applying these and other tools in philosophical contexts must be developed through practice. The following sample of philosophical analysis and series of exercises will help reinforce your understanding of the techniques discussed.

An example of analysis.

Consider the argument "Telepathy is impossible because it cannot be demonstrated by experimental psychology or explained by physics." The following illustration applies the tools described in this chapter to analyzing this argument. We shall be concerned not to argue the case either way in any detail but rather to get a preliminary critical grip on the issue.

①. *What kind of claim is advanced?* First, we should distinguish the thesis ("Telepathy is impossible") from its supporting arguments. It is difficult to determine immediately whether this claim is logical or empirical. On one hand, no conceptual links are apparent, although we may well discover some later. On the other hand, it does not appear to be a straightforward empirical claim, such as "The earth's gravitational pull is greater than that of the moon." So, as is often the case, we shall have to look further to the meanings of the key terms and the nature of the supporting arguments to understand exactly the kind of thesis in question, and in the process, get some idea of why it qualifies as philosophically interesting.

②. *What is the meaning of key terms?* The proponent cannot mean that telepathy is *logically* impossible, for there is no inherent logical contradiction or inconceivability in the idea of telepathy. Therefore, he must mean *empirically* impossible, although we may have to qualify this sense later. That there are two different supporting arguments, one concerning the *evidence* for telepathy (psychology), the other concerning its *nature* (physics), suggests also that two different senses of 'telepathy' are at stake. Accordingly, we might define it as "one person's knowing another's mental states without reliance on normal sensory perception" or as "the transmission of some type of energy from one person's brain to another's." In which sense is telepathy impossible?

③ *Are the supporting arguments valid?* Certainly, from "Telepathy cannot be experimentally demonstrated" (in the former of the above senses), it does not follow that "Telepathy is impossible, that is, cannot possibly be true." The argument can, however, be made provisionally valid once we isolate the questionable assumption on which it seems to be based — namely, that to be possibly true, telepathy must be experimentally verifiable —

and make that an additional premise. This would give us the following *modus tollens* argument form:

1. *If* telepathy is possibly true, *then* it must be experimentally verifiable.
2. But telepathy cannot be experimentally verified.
3. Hence, telepathy is not possibly true, that is, is impossible.

④ *Are the premises true?* The first premise is not an empirical truth but instead is the consequence of an even more fundamental assumption regarding the nature of knowledge. The second premise is an inductive generalization which, in all likelihood, is much too strong for the evidence. From the fact that a relative handful of investigators over the past several decades *do not happen* to have produced definite "proof" of telepathy, we are in a poor position to infer that it *cannot* be reasonably confirmed in the future. Notice, moreover, what happens to the preceding argument if we substitute "has not been verified" for "cannot be verified" in the second premise. When we do this, the second premise ceases to be a denial of the consequent (the phrase following 'then') in the first premise; "has not been verified" is perfectly consistent with "must be verifi*able*." Once this change is made, the conclusion does not follow from the premises.

⑤ *Are the assumptions correct?* The first premise of the supporting argument is the consequence of an even more fundamental assumption, that verifiability is a necessary condition of any belief's possibly being true. But is science the only road to truth? Many beliefs, for example, those about the existence of a God, may well be true yet incapable of scientific confirmation.

The more immediately pressing issue concerns whether telepathy by its very nature might involve a partial exception to the rules of scientific method, in particular the fruitful assumption that *repeatability* is a necessary condition of experimental confirmation. In studies of telepathy, some subjects produce very high test scores. But they seem unable to keep up the good work consistently in the long run. So, should the requirement of repeatability be lifted or at least modified in this case? We begin to see why telepathy is of some philosophical interest. For example, a question arises about the incompatibility between telepathy and the requirement of repeatability. Consequently, this is not an empirical issue but rather one about the nature and limits of empirical knowledge — about what kinds of beliefs must by their nature be excluded from, or included in, these limits.

(6) *Are the consequences of the thesis or its arguments plausible?* Some proponents of the view that telepathy is impossible support their case by citing the highly implausible consequences of assuming that it *is* possible. Let us consider the argument from physics that telepathy cannot be explained. If telepathy were the case, then some of the fundamental laws of physics, for example, the conservation of energy, would be violated. But this result would be preposterous, since those laws are some of the most well-established principles in the history of science. Hence, telepathy cannot be the case. Note that the trouble here is not merely the "mystery" of telepathy, that is, the fact that we cannot seem to find a possible explanation for it. Rather, we know enough about it to surmise that, if it exists, the mechanisms involved are fundamentally incompatible with some of the principles that made possible the phenomenal progress of physics. Here again is an issue in the philosophy of science, a question about the conditions under which established laws should be modified or abandoned to accommodate new evidence; it is not an issue that can be resolved in the laboratory.

Those who argue for the existence of telepathy suggest another, quite different philosophical implication. They admit the conceptual incompatibility of telepathy and many of the laws of physics. They point out, however, that given the formidable (though not decisive) accumulation of positive experimental results, the logical consequence of that incompatibility is not that telepathy is impossible but rather that it must operate by mechanisms (such as "psychic energy") that are outside the domain of physics as we now know it. In other words, laboratory support for telepathy conjoined with the impossibility of explaining it by postulating some type of physical energy (for example, electromagnetic waves) logically suggests some form of dualism. Telepathy, its proponents may argue, implies that persons have minds distinct from their brains and capable of surviving the death of their bodies.

(7) *Are any issues begged?* The distinction between two senses of 'telepathy' (noted in the discussion of key terms) is particularly relevant for the possibility of question-begging. Some persons argue, for instance, that since telepathy in the sense of "a transmission of physical energy" is out of the question, then experiments that purport to show its existence in the other sense

of "reading another's mind" must also be written off as cases of mistaken statistics, poor experimental conditions, fraud, or lucky guessing. In the case of the last difficulty, it potentially begs the issue to hold that individuals who have on numerous occasions achieved odds-against-chance scores of a billion to one must have just been lucky. Scores in this range, in other contexts at least, are normally indicative of genuine ability, not luck.

⑧ *How adequate is the thesis?* The demand for a more adequate frame of reference often arises when two apparently conflicting beliefs for which there is evidence cannot be reconciled within an existing framework. This is perhaps the case with the conflict between present-day experimental evidence for telepathy and the seeming inability to account for it within the theoretical scope of physics. Isn't a wider framework required, wherein one would not be forced into the dubious position of logically excluding telepathy from the class of possible facts on the basis of empirical considerations? Of course, when we suggest the need for a framework *within* which we can place the theoretical principles of science and telepathy, we are going beyond science to the realm of metaphysics. We have reached the point where analysis gives way to the demand for constructive speculation.

Exercises.

The following exercises in philosophical analysis will help to increase your facility in applying the critical tools discussed in this chapter. Some passages are intentionally of no particular philosophical interest and are included to make it easier to apply the relevant tool. Analyzing other passages will require guidance from your instructor. A single passage may suffer from several defects and should be analyzed accordingly. In many passages, a correct response will require that you first clarify the meaning of key terms before applying the relevant critical question.

Answers to selected problems (indicated by an asterisk) are given at the back of this text.

I.   In the following groups of sentences, determine what type of claim (empirical, definitional, etc.) is advanced.

   A.   (1)   Persons deprived of any chance to achieve happiness cease to care about living.

(2)   You cannot find a happy man who thinks only of himself.

(3)   Happiness is the basis of all adequate moral standards.

(4)   There are only two classes of persons, the happy and the nonhappy.

(5)   Happiness is nothing other than having one's desires fulfilled.

B.   (1)   Who am I?
        (2)   What am I?
        (3)   Do I exist?
        (4)   Can I do this?
        (5)   'I' means "the person here, now."

C.   (1)   Because they merely generalize facts of human psychology, existentialists cannot be called philosophers.
        (2)   Philosophy is love of wisdom.
        (3)   Philosophical problems cannot be solved by experiments.
        (4)   Philosophers are usually intelligent persons.
        (5)   Philosophy is completely irrelevant to today's problems.

D.   (1)   Some words have no meaning.
        (2)   In order to be true or false, a sentence must be meaningful.
        (3)   They had a totally meaningless relationship.
        (4)   The meaning of a term is the use to which it is put in a language.
        (5)   The sentence "God does not exist" has no meaning.

E.   (1)   Any man who treats women merely as sexual objects is a male chauvinist pig.
        (2)   Sexual intercourse is copulation.
        (3)   Sex is immoral when its participants are irresponsible.
        (4)   One can't be a puritan and enjoy sex.
        (5)   Too much sex is abnormal.

II.   Evaluate each of the following definitions according to the method of counterexample. In the case of reformative definitions supported by a brief argument, you may wish to consider whether those arguments are sound enough to override your counterexamples.

    A.   Hippies are long-haired dissidents.

    B.   God is a limited and imperfect being, since if He were perfect, He would not have created a world in which evil is so plentiful.

    C.   A philosophical problem is a problem for which science has not yet found the answer.

    *D.   A cause is any event that regularly precedes another event.

    E.   Virtue is nothing other than happiness, because to be virtuous is habitually to do the right thing; doing the right thing is for one's own good; and whatever is for one's good ultimately results in personal happiness.

    *F.   Knowing something means believing it sincerely and strongly.

    *G.   A lie is a misstatement.

    H.   An impeachable offense is any offense that, if perpetrated by someone other than the president of the United States, would be subject to criminal indictment.

    I.   Justice is paying off one's friends and/or punishing one's enemies.

III.   Test the validity of the following arguments by the method of counterexample or by comparison with a valid argument form. (Note: Some arguments may not fit the few forms discussed in this chapter.)

A.   1. If conclusive proofs are possible in logic, then they are also possible in mathematics.

      2. Conclusive proofs are not possible in mathematics.

      3. Hence, they are not possible in logic.

B.   1. For those who believe in God no proof of His existence is necessary.

      2. For those who do not believe in God no proof is possible.

      3. Hence, for those persons who believe or do not believe in God, all proofs of His existence are either unnecessary or impossible.

*C   1. If any argument has all true premises and a false conclusion, then it is invalid.

      2. Jones's argument has all true premises and a false conclusion.

      3. Therefore, Jones's argument is invalid.

D.   1. Our intellects either impose static, artificial categories on the flow of experience or they don't.

      2. If they do, then we cannot know that experience flows.

      3. But we know that experience flows.

      4. So out intellects must not impose static, artificial categories on experience, after all.

E.   1. Some biologists believe that mothers with large families on welfare should be sterilized.

      2. All defenders of civil liberties reject that belief.

      3. Hence, no defenders of civil liberties are biologists.

IV. On what potentially questionable assumptions do the following passages appear to rest?

    A. America: Love it or leave it!

    *B. If Congress would just pass more social legislation, we would eliminate crime.

    C. Abortions are perfectly moral because women have a right to control their own bodies.

    *D. Anyone old enough to fight for his country is old enough to vote.

    E. Of course Truman's decision to use nuclear weapons was justified — think of the lives it saved!

    F. Because the dominant age group of Americans is eighteen to thirty-five years, government policies should reflect the values of persons in that age bracket.

    G. Since physiologists have begun to correlate with great precision the occurrence of certain states of our nervous systems with the occurrence of certain experiences, proof that the mind and the brain are the same thing is not far off.

    H. Judaism must be a true religion, for it has stood the test of time.

    *I. Those who have not served in the military should not be allowed to criticize publicly its rules and regulations.

V. What potentially questionable or self-defeating consequences appear to follow from the following passages?

    A. Everyone should lie.

    *B. All generalizations are false.

C.   Depression is nothing but behaving in certain seemingly "depressed" ways.

D.   A person is free to define any word as he pleases.

E.   No state of the universe or any part thereof is causally related to an earlier or later state of the universe.

*F.   Everyone ought to pursue only those courses of action that are in his own self-interest.

G.   If we could construct an entity that looked and behaved just like a regular person, we would still have no reason to believe that it was a conscious, much less self-conscious, being.

*H.   Time sometimes passes very slowly.

I.   Philosophers ought to give us reasons for being rational.

VI.   Suggest possible defects of adequacy in the following passages by citing counterexamples.

*A.   Where there is a will, there is also a way.

B.   Psychology is concerned exclusively with establishing lawlike relations between certain types of behavior and the causes leading to such behavior.

*C.   The purpose of dramatic acting is to induce in the spectators an identification with, or a revulsion for, the characters.

D.   One knows something only if he cannot possibly be mistaken about it.

*E.   Once we learn the causes of persons' believing the things they do, philosophy will be reduced to merely a historical survey of past philosophers' beliefs.

F.   The central difference between science and philos-
        ophy is that science concerns itself with the
        observable world only, and philosophy concerns
        itself with abstract, unobservable entities.

G.   A man is not educated unless he is trained to cope
        with the cold, cruel world.

H.   Something is better than nothing.

I.   It is better to have loved and lost than never to
        have loved at all.

VII.   Determine which of the following arguments beg the issue
        and explain why.

*A.   The laws against homosexuality are good, since
        homosexuality is immoral and immoral practices
        ought to be outlawed.

B.   Miracles are impossible because they violate the
        laws of nature.

C.   Since our senses deceive us sometimes, it is possible
        that they deceive us all the time. So our senses are
        not to be trusted as sources of knowledge.

D.   Since persons may be taught to respond to a single
        color stimulus by saying, for example, "That is
        red," yet actually perceive a different color, there
        is no way to know for sure whether the colors we
        all perceive are the same.

E.   Jim spoke with an angel last night, and I believe
        him, because nobody who speaks with angels
        would ever lie.

*F.   Since general agreement does not appear possible
        in judging works of art, beauty must be in the eye
        of the beholder.

G.   Steve is antiunion because unions so often force a

small businessman into bankruptcy. But Steve is mistaken for the simple reason that if small businessmen cannot pay the living wage unions request, then small businessmen ought to be forced out of business.

H.   Anyone who attempts to define 'philosophy' other than etymologically is doomed to fail, since no one has yet succeeded in doing so.

*I.   Bertrand Russell once suggested that the earth *could* have come into being five minutes ago, just as it is now or only slightly changed. But that's preposterous because carbon-14 tests show the earth to be millions of years old.

Notes

1.   For a useful and engaging survey of the uses and abuses of reason in nonphilosophical contexts, consult Howard Kahane, *Logic and Contemporary Rhetoric: The Use of Reason in Everyday Life* (Belmont, Calif.: Wadsworth, 1971). Many of the topics treated in this chapter are discussed in Irving Copi, *Introduction to Logic*, 4th ed. (New York: Macmillan, 1972). A readable and practical text for the beginning student wishing to gain a working knowledge of techniques for analyzing concepts is John Wilson's *Thinking with Concepts* (New York: Cambridge University Press, 1969). For the advanced student, more technical expositions and applications of philosophical methods are found in Samuel Gorovitz and Ron Williams, *Philosophical Analysis: An Introduction to Its Language and Techniques*, 2nd ed. (New York: Random House, 1965); and Ian G. MacGreal, *Analyzing Philosophical Arguments* (Scranton, Pa.: Chandler, 1967).

2.   The term being defined is sometimes referred to as the *definiendum* and the expression used to define it as the *definiens*.

3.   You should be careful not to confuse the notion of a logical or conceptual consequence in philosophy with that of an empirical consequence in science. Both forms are closely tied to hypothetical, or "if-then," reasoning. In philosophy, for example, one might encounter the thesis that *if* God is morally perfect, *then* there should be no evil in the world He created. In science, on the other hand, a commonly encountered hypothesis is that *if* air has weight, *then* barometers should measure lower air pressure at higher altitudes. The similarity begins to fade rapidly here, however. For the consequences of a scientific hypothesis, you will recall, take the form of predicted observable events verifiable at some point in the future. The consequences of a

philosophical hypothesis, in contrast, are conceptual inferences wherein one apprehends a logical relation between two or more claims. In the above example, the relation between the concepts of 'moral perfection' and 'evil' is one of logical incompatibility.

4.   This is also true in science. But the adequacy of a scientific theory or law is usually judged according to its *explanatory power*, that is, its ability to generate accurate, testable consequences. And in this sense, explanatory power is not a criterion of adequacy for philosophical theories.

Chapter IV

Is Philosophical Progress Possible?

Developing skill in using the critical tools of philosophy is not an easy task. At some point you may even ask yourself if it is worth the trouble. That is, will developing critical reasoning abilities enable you to solve problems and to discover the truth? Do professional philosophers actually make progress in their investigations? Can you expect to "get anywhere" in your first course?

The temptation to answer these questions in the negative may emerge as you analyze conflicting answers to long-debated questions. You may find yourself inclined to claim, perhaps, that philosophy is merely a matter of semantics or else simply a process of rationalizing beliefs to which we are already emotionally attached. The purpose of this chapter is to respond to some of the skepticism concerning the possibility of philosophical progress. We shall be doing elementary philosophizing as we apply some of the critical tools already described.

Philosophy is not merely an exercise in semantics.

The argument that philosophical progress is undermined by "quibbling over words" may be stated as follows. To begin with, to make progress in philosophy, we must at least partially resolve some outstanding issues. These solutions in turn require that we forge common definitions for the key terms involved in those issues. Sooner or later, the answer to such questions as "Can persons survive the death of their bodies?" and "Is pornography a legitimate art form?" will depend on how we define 'person' and 'art form'. Different philosophers, however, often define the key terms of any given issue in different and even inconsistent ways, usually in a manner that will ultimately support the truth of their own views. If a philosopher believes, for example, that persons can survive the death of their bodies, then he will define 'person' in a way to insure that possibility. A person, he might hold, is essentially a spiritual entity distinct from his physical body. In the end, a discussion of immortality will boil down to insisting that a certain definition of 'person' is really the correct one. In such a case, skeptics argue, the possibility of philosophical progress is remote.

This argument raises a number of implicit issues, the most important of which is the mistaken assumption on which it rests. To someone who attempts to undercut the potential progress of a philosophical discussion by claiming, "It all depends on how you define your terms," the most disarming response is simply, "Of course it does." But from this it does not follow that the discussion should come to an end. On the contrary, it is usually just getting started. Given any two competing definitions, the next question is "What *reasons* are there for preferring one definition to the other?" One person's definition is not always as good as another's. Further debate must determine which is more adequate.

The assumption behind the view that progress comes to an end once we put our respective definitions on the table is that all definitions are purely arbitrary. Most definitions in philosophy, however, are reportive and/or reformative. And both of these types, you will recall from earlier discussion, require further evaluation by referring to the appropriate criteria. The possibility of progress at this juncture is still an open question to be decided by the merits of the ensuing debate. The view that philosophy is merely an exercise in semantics, then, fails as a serious challenge to the possibility of philosophical progress.

The choice between competing theories is not arbitrary.

Skeptics sometimes argue that philosophical commitment is arbitrary in the following way. For our commitment to a certain thesis to be rationally justified, that thesis must be relatively freed from serious objections and supported with sound arguments. It seems, however, that most of the solutions to various problems can be supported with good arguments, and in addition, it seems that they nearly all suffer from serious objections. Hence, selecting this or that theory as *the* solution, from the standpoint of rational justification, is arbitrary — a matter of personal preference. And if the choice between competing theories is rationally arbitrary, then any progress in philosophy must be illusory.

The Achilles' heel of this argument is the mistaken assumption that philosophical truth is an all-or-nothing proposition. The skeptic insists that in order to be rationally justifiable, a philosophical thesis must be supported with conclusive arguments; he demands certainty. When it seems that certainty cannot be had, since nearly all philosophical claims are subject to some objections, the skeptic concludes that the view in question is no better or worse than its competitors.

For persons searching for eternal truth and total freedom from doubt, philosophy will not provide a comfortable home. But it does not follow that there are no reasons for preferring one theory over its rivals. The rational acceptability of any given philosophical thesis is primarily a matter of *degree*. There is much ground between absolute certainty and complete skepticism. For you to avoid unnecessary frustration with philosophy, this is an important fact to keep in mind.

Suppose we could show that one of two competing views about what makes an object a work of art is supported by invalid arguments, relies on arbitrary assumptions and definitions, and entails self-defeating consequences, whereas the other suffers only from defects of adequacy. Surely we would say that the latter is rationally preferable to the former. Of course, the catch is that one must *show* that the view in question actually suffers from the difficulties he envisages and also be prepared for a counterattack on his criticisms. But this is simply part of the challenge of philosophy.

Part of the plausibility of the all-or-nothing assumption stems from a misconception about the purpose of philosophy. Its purpose is not, as some may assume, a mad scramble to stake out a series of static truths that, when once achieved, will enable us to rest on our laurels and cease to think about philosophical problems. It is rather a cumulative, ongoing activity in which each generation of philosophers attempts to build on the insights of their predecessors and to avoid their mistakes. Within the context of this activity, tentative conclusions are continually refined and modified, sometimes even abandoned, in an effort to achieve a greater degree of truth. For these reasons, your introductory course will help you start doing philosophy on your own, not simply memorizing facts.

Since the view that philosophical commitment is arbitrary is so pervasive, let us briefly examine it from a different perspective. Beginning students of philosophy sometimes advance the following claim: "Although for Smith, theory X is false, X is nevertheless true *for me*. And from our own points of view, each of us is correct!" Consider a consequence of this position. Suppose that theory X is that the earth is flat. Now if both Smith and you are correct, then the earth must actually be both flat and not flat (spherical). But the same thing cannot be both flat and spherical, so the position that generated this contradiction must be mistaken.

Positions that lead to contradictions are usually based on faulty assumptions. The culprit in this case is the failure to distinguish between the *belief* and the *truth* of that belief. By distinguishing between truth and belief, we are able to avoid the consequence that two inconsistent beliefs, merely by virtue of their being sincerely held, are both true.

This distinction accounts for the necessary role that evidence plays in making rational commitments. The evidence supporting the belief that the earth is spherical far outweighs the evidence available for the belief that it is not; mere belief does not support either the truth or falsity of a proposition. Seen in this light, the most plausible interpretation of "Theory X is true *for me*" is simply "I believe X." The qualification *for me* does not magically transform mere belief into true belief. If it did, the concept of evidence would become superfluous, and the distinction between rational commitment and arbitrary whim would collapse. To retain this distinction, one must work his way through the evidence, not circumvent the process of rational investigation by declaring that the view in question is "true for me"!

Philosophers do agree.

Probably the most common variation of the skeptical challenge to philosophical progress is that philosophers seldom, if ever, agree with one another. They seem to present no unified front, no conclusive set of facts for one to memorize. To be sure, one does find general agreement among philosophers of a given school or persuasion concerning the solution to a certain problem. But there always seem to be others who disagree with that solution. In every period, philosophers continually call into question the arguments and theories advanced by their predecessors. So if progress is equated with agreement among philosophers, then it seems an unrealistic ideal. There are two responses to this argument: (1) it is false because it admits of many counter-examples; (2) it rests on some muddled assumptions concerning the need to agree in order to make philosophical progress. Let us consider each of these responses separately.

General agreement among philosophers occurs in several different areas. In the first place, by nearly unanimous consent, a great deal of progress has been made in the degree of precision and perspective introduced into the formulation of different philosophical puzzles. For example, a question typical of Socrates is "What is the essence of beauty?" These days, such a formulation tends to be rejected in favor of an attempt to answer the more specific questions it implies. Is this question a request for the criteria by which we distinguish beautiful from nonbeautiful objects? Is there an essence of beauty in general, or merely different criteria to be applied to different classes of art objects? For example, must all art forms embody a theme or message? And what, after all, would the "essence" of something be? By what standards would one know that he had grasped it? These questions, though difficult, are more manageable than the original formulation, and to this extent enhance the possibility of progress.

Second, there is general consensus among philosophers that many theories are simply wrong. For example, the sixteenth-century philosopher Hobbes argued that all men are by nature selfishly motivated and incapable of putting the interests of others ahead of their own — unless, of course, they felt that doing so would actually improve their own long-range interests. This view, known as psychological egoism, has been subjected to devastating criticism. So there is what we may call "negative" progress in philosophy. Whether or not the definitive answer is ever established with respect to a given issue, the rejection of extremely unlikely or false alternatives represents a concrete step in that direction.

Third, there is universal agreement among philosophers concerning many of the *methods* of correct argumentation. Showing that a certain thesis entails self-defeating consequences, begs the issue, and rests on invalid arguments, for example, are unanimously accepted techniques of philosophical investigation. Of course, opinions vary regarding the proper total approach to a given problem. For instance, is the most fruitful point of departure to rely primarily on a rigorous *analysis* of the meaning of key concepts as they are found in our language? Or should philosophical method involve more disciplined *speculation* — an attempt to express novel views of the world through introducing new, more specialized concepts that incorporate scientific facts as a foundation? These differences regarding the broader facets of philosophical method, however, are not necessarily inconsistent with each other. Given the diversity of philosophical subject matter, there is no reason to suppose in advance that the issues must yield to one and only one method.

In summary, there does exist much agreement within the philosophical enterprise. Nevertheless, for the beginning student, the areas of widespread disagreement still pose a serious challenge to making philosophical progress. Our next response to the skeptics, then, should focus on the mistaken assumption that agreement is a necessary condition of philosophical progress.

Suppose that philosophers on the whole did agree on the correct answer to a wide variety of questions. Would common agreement entail that these answers were actually the correct ones? Certainly not! The history of thought is pregnant with instances of heretics pointing out the inadequacies or even falsehoods latent in the prevailing majority opinion. This is as true of science as it is of philosophy. One need only recall Copernicus's heretical suggestion that the earth was not the center of the universe. Although each generation may believe that it is closer to the truth than preceding generations, belief itself does not make a thesis true. To validate a thesis, we must evaluate the reasons offered in support of it, be they scientific, philosophical, or whatever.

The conclusion we may derive from these considerations, then, is that just as agreement in belief does not entail that the thesis in question is true, a lack of agreement does not mean that none of the disputants has made significant progress in ascertaining the truth. Irrespective of agreement or disagreement, truth can be determined only by rationally analyzing the supporting arguments.

The mistaken identification of progress with agreement in philosophy is often caused by the failure to distinguish between *good* reasons and *persuasive* reasons. The two do not necessarily coincide. A persuasive argument may actually contain many fallacies, and a thoroughly sound argument may fail to produce many converts. For example, the argument that since evaluations of art differ, then beauty must be in the eye of the beholder is persuasive for many persons. However, it is not sound. Of course, the argument that generates the most agreement is the most persuasive. But since persuasive arguments are not necessarily good arguments, the ensuing agreement is not automatically a sign that progress has been made toward reaching the most rationally defensible position. That can be determined, once again, only through a careful analysis of each case, not by an appeal to widespread agreement.

Philosophical theories are not merely rationalizations of personal belief.

Another challenge to the possibility of philosophical progress is the claim that the choice between competing theories is ultimately determined by an individual's conditioning and natural tendencies. Skeptics often hold that the use of argument in philosophy is really a process of rationalizing the beliefs, commitments, and even unconscious tendencies already inherent in us. And since these various subjective factors determine our acceptance of new and better theories, the notion of objective progress in philosophy is an illusion.

A common form of this skeptical doubt is illustrated by the use of ad hominem arguments (that is, attacking a person's character or personal circumstances rather than his arguments) and in the tendency to predict and evaluate a man's philosophy in relation to the kind of personality he exhibits. We may hear it argued, for example, that since Jones is an insecure person, he is incapable of evaluating fairly any philosophical position that advocates the periodic overthrow of authority, the importance of change, and the relativity of morals — in other words, the very factors that would make his life even more insecure. A more advanced version of doubting the possibility of objectivity is based on the observation that philosophers of superior intellect, extensive training, and unquestioned integrity differ radically and consistently on many important issues. Given their equally superior qualities, how else can we explain their disagreements except by referring to perhaps as yet undiscovered (or poorly understood) differences of personal psychology?

There are two standard responses to this line of argumentation. First, the psychology behind a person's commitment to a certain theory is irrelevant to evaluating the arguments supporting it, and only the latter activity is of interest to the philosopher. Citing various psychological factors that may be instrumental in establishing philosophical commitment does not render the theory in question either less important or less in need of critical examination. Second, the hypothesis of "psychological conditioning factors" is overly speculative (if not false), since it would be practically impossible to specify all the factors leading to the adoption of any given view. If these responses are not necessarily persuasive from your standpoint as a student of philosophy, a different approach might be to assume that the hypothesis of psychological conditioning is both initially relevant and true, and then show that the consequences for philosophical progress are not as damaging as might be imagined.

The first important consequence is that if it is true, the hypothesis of conditioning applies to everyone, not only to philosophers; no person escapes conditioning. Previous conditioning should therefore taint the claims of art critic, mathematician, theologian, lawyer, statesman, and physicist alike. But in practice it does not, at least not in any systematic, across-the-board sense. To take a rather crude example, nobody questions the thesis that human beings evolved from lower forms of life solely on the grounds that its proponents are psychologically deviant because they have a pathological attachment to animals. Despite his psychological quirks, the biologist has good reasons for the theory of evolution.

At this point lies the difficulty. For philosophers, too, support their positions with reasons. And whether or not these reasons are sound can be determined only by carefully analyzing the arguments themselves. Their potential defects, just as the potential merits of a scientific hypothesis, have to be *shown*. Wholesale rejection on essentially psychological grounds would be arbitrary. The weakness of the psychological conditioning hypothesis is that it covers too much territory. Taken to its extreme, all intellectual inquiry would reduce to a psychoanalytic or behavioral study of the causes that determine the beliefs to be accepted in each discipline. The fact that this does not happen means that each claim to truth, philosophical claims included, must be evaluated on its own merits and using the criteria relevant to the area in which it is made.

A second response to the skeptical hypothesis of psychological conditioning is that, even if true, there is no reason to suppose that any influence is one-directional. That is, reason can influence, even change, our fundamental beliefs, emotional attachments, and attitudes, as well as be influenced by them. Carefully considering all the arguments for and against a given thesis can produce personal conversion. Indeed, there are many potential psychological consequences of being faced with a particularly forceful philosophical argument. Consider, for example, the possible ramifications for a man who devotes his life to "fighting Communists," only to become convinced at a later date of the plausibility of many Marxian ideas.

With respect to any given problem, we seldom know how the psychological influence will work. Usually the only way to find out is to become intellectually involved. The assumption of those who attempt to reduce rational commitment and progress in philosophy to a psychological model is that the influence is *only* by feelings and attitudes on the use of reason. Yet some of these attitudes may themselves be ingrained in our character partly as a result of arguments with which we are confronted. For example, the argument "If God had meant the poor to be economic equals with the rich he would have created them with the ability to become rich" at one time helped establish the attitude that poverty was inevitable. Seen in this light, the distinction between the rational and nonrational aspects of personal commitment becomes a little blurred. The formulation of arguments and the use of reason can be both influenced by, and further influence, many of our personal feelings and attitudes. So the possibility of progressing toward a rationally defensible resolution of any problem, philosophical ones included, remains an open question — despite the psychology of its proponent.

Why be rational?

The preceding discussion has attempted to show that the pursuit of philosophical truth through critical argumentation is not undercut by the skeptical challenges we have surveyed. But the attitude these challenges express can be directed toward the assumption of rationality itself. Just why must one be rational? The answers given to this question will naturally depend on how it is interpreted. Not surprisingly, there are several alternatives.

The question "Why be rational?" might express a request for a justification of the use of reason. As such, the question would be unanswerable, since it would be applicable to all the reasons given in response. No matter what one answered, the skeptic could respond with a request for a further justification of the one just offered, and so on, ad infinitum. In contrast, if the scope of the question is limited to only philosophical issues, then the question might be interpreted simply as expressing a lack of interest in critically investigating any philosophical issues.

Assuming one is interested in a philosophical issue, a closely related interpretation of the question "Why be rational?" is that it asks why the use of reason may be expected to settle anything — or, worse yet, that it expresses the belief that it cannot. Such a negative interpretation falls within the range of an overriding issue of this chapter. To isolate this issue, consider the following claims often encountered in lay discussions of philosophical issues.

1. That's just your opinion!
2. It's all a matter of definition, anyway!
3. He'll only argue for what he's been taught!
4. Well, *that*, of course, is a philosophical issue!
5. We'll never agree!
6. Being rational won't get us anywhere!
7. Theory X is true *for me*, and that's what counts!

Such statements express distinct, yet partially overlapping, themes. Common to each of them is an implicit "Let's stop here!" Their effect, if not intent, is to cut off further dialogue. It is amazing how often the use of such a phrase as "That's a philosophical issue" or "That's a value judgment" forces a silence on a conversation or else rapidly changes the topic or argumentative strategy. More important, using such phrases also has the effect of discrediting the competing theory while generating respect for one's own view. When cornered in a discussion concerning some moral or social issue, one of the most effective, yet misguided, defenses is simply to accuse one's opponent of dabbling in unprovable philosophical arguments, of bias, or of making value judgments. It's as if to say, "Your views are no better than the words used to express them and are certainly no better than mine!"

This chapter has attempted to show that these maneuvers do not deserve the favorable reception they often receive. It is simply not true, for instance, that one person's definitions or philosophical arguments are always as good (or as bad) as another's. Two additional responses to the skeptic remain, however — one based on an appeal to self-interest, the other on an appeal to consistency.

Let's first consider the matter of consistency. It has probably occurred to many of you that the topic of this chapter, "Is philosophical progress possible?" is itself a philosophical issue. And therein lies the rub. If the total rejection of philosophy is to be anything more than an arbitrary decree, then it must be based on reasons. Those reasons in turn will be sound only if it can be shown that they do not themselves involve still further philosophical issues. And this is precisely what cannot be shown.

One cannot explicitly reject with consistency the very type of rational involvement implicitly assumed in that rejection. To reject the possibility of philosophical progress inevitably involves one in doing philosophy.

Let us examine another response to the skeptical challenge, based on an appeal to self-interest. Briefly, the reason that cutting short debate should be avoided is that in the long run, one stands to cheat himself. In a broad sense, it is in your interest to push the defense and criticism of a philosophical theory to its limits. Now, it is easy to illustrate why being rational "pays" in nonphilosophical disciplines — for example, in wiping out cancer by applying scientific methods. It is harder to defend rationality in the case of philosophy because the issues and arguments we encounter there are further removed from goals with which we can easily identify. But there *are* practical results, however strained they may sometimes seem. Intellectual curiosity, peace of mind, moral decision, political commitment, redirecting scientific investigation — all of these can be influenced by the positions we entertain on a variety of philosophical issues. And the only way we can determine what the influence of our philosophical positions is, its extent, and whether our beliefs ought to be changed is through getting on with the business of critical investigation. The attempt to circumvent this task with a "that's-just-your-opinion" approach is a refusal to face the potentially momentous consequences of rational inquiry.

Some may object that the preceding observations mistakenly imply that the pursuit of truth will make one happier when in fact the truth, or at least the most rationally defensible view (to put it more conservatively), sometimes makes persons unhappy. To meet this objection, we must distinguish between one's apparent versus one's real happiness. Of course, anyone can refuse to pursue a rational critique of his own philosophical assumptions regarding science, art, or religion on the grounds that he is happy with those he holds. But the views to which one is instinctively attracted or else has inherited from his culture are not necessarily the ones he will be most comfortable with in the long run. They may eventually lead to so many inconsistencies and absurdities that they must be abandoned. And nobody knows beforehand whether or not he would be happier as a result of calling his philosophical beliefs into question and seriously considering other alternatives. Once again, the only way to determine that is to take the intellectual risk of becoming critically involved.

Chapter V

Writing Philosophy

Preparing to write one's first philosophy essay usually raises a number of important questions. Is this like writing a research paper? Does the instructor just want my opinion about a certain issue? How do I get started? Am I supposed to improve on the views of professional philosophers? The purpose of this chapter is to help you understand what is normally expected when you are asked to write a critical philosophy essay. We will also give you some practical rules to follow as you write your paper.

The nature of a critical philosophy essay.

Unlike the term papers you may have been assigned in courses other than philosophy, the central purpose of a philosophy paper is not usually *reportive;* rather, it is *critical.* Reportive work generally takes two forms: either expressing a personal point of view on an assigned topic, for example, your conception of love; or compiling and organizing the results of laboratory or book research, for example, the economic causes of social unrest. In both forms, one simply presents the facts either as he understands them or as someone else does. Your philosophy instructor may, of course, assign a purely reportive project. However, this chapter deals essentially with critical philosophy papers.

A critical philosophy essay involves much more than simply presenting your own opinions and the views of relevant philosophers on a take-it-or-leave-it basis. Instead, one questions and becomes intellectually involved with his subject matter, taking little for granted. Specifically, there are four primary rules to follow in writing a critical philosophy essay. First, you must *clarify* key ideas. For instance, are the philosophically trouble-

---

This chapter was written in association with Professor Steven M. Sanders of the Department of Philosophy, Bridgewater State College, Bridgewater, Massachusetts.

some terms defined? Are the theories in question exemplified and presented in straightforward language? Second, you must *test* the soundness of arguments given either for or against the theories in question. Are the inferences valid? Are the premises true? Third, you must *evaluate* the theories using some of the methods discussed in Chapter III of this book. Are the assumptions correct? Are the consequences plausible? Fourth, and most important, you must *support* what you assert with reasons. Are your claims backed up with arguments? Do they follow from other claims already established? To summarize, in a reportive paper you organize and pass on others' thoughts, whereas in a critical philosophy essay you think for yourself.

The topic of *support* is especially important. Many students have the tendency to rely on certain illegitimate methods of supporting a position, some of which we noted earlier. For example, you should not support your case merely by (1) labeling it "your own," (2) asserting its superiority over the competition, (3) using ad hominem attacks, or (4) citing an authority (philosophical or scientific) without including any arguments. The views of great philosophers can be questioned. And although citing a scientific authority is usually sufficient to accept certain empirical facts, you will recall from Chapter I that those facts do not entail the truth of any particular philosophical theory. Finally, you should not support your position merely by (5) exemplifying or defining it. These latter tactics tell your reader only *what* you are arguing for, not *why* he should accept it as true. The following passage, which contains no arguments (conclusions derived from premises), illustrates some incorrect methods of supporting a position. (The relevant defect is indicated in parentheses next to the statement.)

> Let me support the view known as ethical relativism. The truth of ethical relativism is shown by the fact that two persons might disagree over the moral rightness of a certain act and, if they are from different cultures or backgrounds, both may be correct (5). Now anyone who denies this is authoritarian (3). Who am I to condemn the Eskimos for leaving their aged relatives on the ice to die? Moreover, anthropologists have been telling us for a long time that ethical relativism is true (4). Finally, the only alternative to ethical relativism is ethical absolutism, and we know absolutism is false (2).

Many students worry about producing a critical philosophy essay because they fear that their labors will be evaluated according to their instructor's personal beliefs. Let us emphasize, however, that your essay will be analyzed on the basis of objective criteria. For example, have you written clearly? Is your case supported with arguments? Have you fairly and accurately presented others' views? Is your essay well organized? Have you attempted to think for yourself instead of just parroting the views of other philosophers? Your essay will not be evaluated on the basis of your personal convictions. Whether or not your instructor agrees with the general position you advance is largely irrelevant. In fact, most instructors of philosophy would prefer that you rationally *support* a theory that they may think is false rather than merely *present* a view that they may believe is true!

Organizing your essay.

Putting together a coherent, well-organized philosophy essay is not a simple and clear-cut task. This section will discuss five organizational strategies that may help you organize your essay. The strategies are: (1) formulating the problem, (2) deciding on a format, (3) incorporating other philosophers' views, (4) presenting a good introduction, and (5) achieving coherence.

Formulating the problem. Critical philosophy essays involve responses to philosophical problems. If it has not been done already, your first task should be to translate the general problem or topic about which you are writing into a specific *question* or *statement.* Suppose, for example, that you are asked to write a critical essay on the problem of evil. You should first ask yourself exactly what questions this problem involves. In the case of the problem of evil, a relevant question would be: "How can God's perfect nature, particularly His moral character, be reconciled with the existence of evil in the world?" Then again, you may wish to focus critical attention on a certain controversial response to that question. If so, this response must be translated into a specific statement, for example, "Man, not God, is responsible for evil through the depraved exercise of his free will," which may then be either attacked or defended. Performing such preliminary "translations" will give you a focal point around which to organize your essay and will help prevent your drifting from the issue during the course of your analysis.

Once you have formulated the specific question or statement with which you will be dealing, you should then clarify the key terms. A lack of clarity in the initial formulation of the problem can affect the organization and direction of your essay. For example, consider the term 'evil' used above. So long as we restrict ourselves to a certain kind of evil, namely, moral evil, such as lying and killing, it is easier to suppose that man is responsible for introducing evil in what was originally a perfect world. However, even if we accept this response at face value and we do not question the assumption of "free will", the restriction to moral evil only partially resolves the problem. Why? Because it does not account for natural evil such as disease. Surely man is not responsible for disease. Wouldn't God remain responsible for natural evil? Answers to questions involving one kind of evil do not automatically transfer to questions involving another kind. Distinguishing between the kinds of evil at the beginning of your analysis would probably require you to limit your investigation to one variety or else to adopt a different strategy that will enable you to reconcile both types of evil with God's moral perfection. Initial clarity greatly improves organizational strategy. (Clarity is discussed in more detail in the next section.)

Having clarified the key terms, you should next think through the assumptions of the question you are attempting to answer and consider how they may influence its formulation and the kinds of answers that might be given. For example, the question "Why did God create the world with so much evil?" tends to lock one into a relatively narrow range of answers, all involving God's *motives*. A natural response that uncritically takes the question at face value is: "Because God *wanted* a testing ground for distinguishing between the worthy and the not so worthy." A critical look at the assumptions of the question, however, might easily have led either to a different formulation or to raising a different issue altogether. The question "Why did God create the world with so much evil?" already presupposes affirmative answers to "Does God exist?"; "Did God create the world?"; "Is God responsible for evil?"; and even "Does evil exist?" If good reasons can be found for answering any of these latter questions in the negative — for example, reasons for concluding that God is not responsible for evil — then the original question about *why* He created a world with evil collapses. You will find it helpful, then, to consider the assumptions implied in your initial formulation of the problem before writing your essay.

Deciding on a format. Closely related to the task of formulating the problem is deciding on an appropriate format for developing your ideas. Probably the most commonly adopted formats are: (1) comparing and contrasting several theories — for example, two attempted resolutions to the problem of evil — with the aim of determining the most adequate among them; (2) criticizing a single theory or argument; (3) defending another philosopher's view against mistaken criticism; and (4) supporting an original theory of your own.

You must decide which format (and these are not the only ones) best suits your interests and abilities. Remember, however, that philosophy is a cumulative activity wherein one comes closer to the truth by avoiding the mistakes of other philosophers. So if you do not know where to begin, the most fruitful strategy for your first essay would probably be to criticize views that seem to you mistaken. Why? Because you already have at your disposal those critical techniques discussed in Chapter III. Asking yourself "Does this argument appear sound?" and "Are the consequences of this view plausible?" enables you to take an important first step in thinking for yourself.[1] Also, by avoiding the criticisms applicable to implausible views, the lines along which your own thesis must be developed will emerge naturally.

Incorporating other philosophers' views. In organizing your paper, you may find yourself asking; "How am I supposed to improve on the theories of philosophers who have spent their lives thinking about these issues? Even where I think one philosopher is wrong, it seems that all I can do is quote another philosopher to support my contention. I have thought about the issue and in my opinion, philosopher X's arguments are correct, so here they are!" The beginning student in philosophy is not expected to revolutionize philosophical thinking. Rather, as indicated earlier, your instructor is interested primarily in getting you to begin thinking for yourself. Moreover, so long as you give credit where it is due, it is natural that you will use the arguments of other philosophers. No writer on philosophical problems works in a vacuum.

Most important, the above quandary rests on a false assumption. Exercising one's own problem-solving abilities is not incompatible with supplementing them with other philosophers' theories and arguments. Often, your paper will blend or synthesize your thinking with the views about which you have read. For example, you may defend *another* person's theory against unsound criticism with your *own* arguments. Other possible blends are: (1) restating a philosopher's argument or theory in a clearer, more incisive, way; (2) applying that argument or theory to areas not discussed by its original proponent; (3) admitting the view is mistaken in places but attempting to remedy those deficiencies and thus produce a modified view.

Presenting a good introduction. Once you have thought through the problem, determined the general conclusions you wish to argue for, and decided on a format for developing your ideas, you should be ready to express the results of your preliminary investigation in a good introduction. A good introduction clearly sets out (1) the problem to which you will address yourself; (2) what you intend to show, for example, that one theory is preferable to another; and (3) how you propose to do this, for example, by showing that one theory rests on highly questionable assumptions.

A good introduction has several virtues. First, it helps keep your essay on the right track. That is, if you commit yourself to showing that a certain thesis is false, then that is what you must do. The chances are much greater that your essay will lack coherence and direction if you do not spell out your commitments in advance. Second, it gives the reader some assurance that you know what you are about to undertake. There is no exact format for good introductions. The following paragraph, however, illustrates each of the three characteristics of a good introduction.

> In his novel about a behaviorally engineered utopia, *Walden II,* B. F. Skinner claims through one of its central characters that if man is free then a science of human behavior is impossible. Since Skinner believes that a science of psychology is possible, he draws the inference that man is not free. While his thesis may be supportable on other grounds, I propose to demonstrate in this paper that Skinner's reasons for denying human freedom are not persuasive. After presenting his view in more detail, I shall argue that his case rests on two faulty assumptions concerning the nature of freedom and the purpose of science. A science of psychology, we shall see, is quite compatible with human freedom.

Achieving coherence. Many undergraduate papers in philosophy suffer from a lack of coherence and incisiveness — what we may characterize as a "drifting" phenomenon. Your reader becomes puzzled over where you are and what you are doing. Undefined terms appear from nowhere. Arguments having little or no indication of what they are supposed to show are presented. The same point is rehashed in five different ways. Examples are inserted randomly. Too much territory is covered in a single sentence or paragraph. Too much writing is devoted to points not essential to one's case or perhaps to saying nothing. These are just some of the manifestations of drifting.

Of course, this phenomenon is by no means unique either to philosophy papers or to students alone. It tends to occur more frequently in students' philosophy papers, however, because of the relative novelty of the subject matter and the great degree of intellectual discipline required to produce a good philosophy essay. After you have written your first draft, therefore, go through it again, sentence by sentence, paragraph by paragraph, and ask yourself the following questions. What is the relevance of this passage, and does it clearly fit here? Is the passage an essential link in my argument? Is it used to clarify? Does it tell the reader where I am and where I'm going? If it is an argument, is its relevance to what I'm trying to show clear? Does this sentence add anything to the substance of my essay? Does my introduction get to the point? Your responses to these questions may entail rewriting or deleting some passages. Doing so, however, will help greatly to tighten the organization of your paper.

Achieving clarity.

Developing a sound organization is essential for communicating your ideas effectively in a philosophy essay. Achieving clarity is also necessary for effective communication. These ingredients are closely related. A well-organized essay contributes greatly to the overall clarity (and persuasiveness) of your essay. Our concern in this section, however, is primarily with individual words and sentences. We shall consider the following areas: first, insuring that key terms clearly express the ideas they are supposed to convey; second, using examples properly; and third, improving your style of writing.

Clearly expressing your ideas. Achieving clarity of written expression presupposes that one has a clear idea about what he is writing. If you do not understand the point you attempt to get across, you can hardly expect your reader to be enlightened, no matter how pleasing your style of expression may be. There is no foolproof procedure for gaining this prerequisite understanding. Rereading your sources, participating in "think sessions" with your friends, conferring with your instructor, and applying some of the critical questions discussed in Chapter III, however, should help.

Once you know what you wish to say, you will want to consider how you can communicate your ideas most effectively. If you do not express yourself clearly, your reader will usually assume that you do not understand well the topic you are writing about. Initial clarity of expression is always preferable to after-the-fact debates over whether one really understood the subject about which he was writing. Most instructors are unmoved by such exhortations from students as: "Come on, now, you know what I meant!" To which you are most likely to hear in response: "Well, why didn't you say what you meant?" Following are a few rules of thumb that will help to insure a clear statement of your ideas.

First, avoid vagueness, particularly of key terms and sentences. A vague expression is one whose meaning is not clear and that fails to specify exactly to what objects or circumstances it should be applied. Vague ideas are "rough" ideas. For example, a vague idea of 'democracy' is "a political system in which the people have something to say about how they are governed." Although this conception of democracy is not incorrect, it needs considerable refinement. Who, for instance, are "the people" — those educated enough to vote intelligently or sufficiently well off to pay taxes without going hungry? Are we talking about a majority of the people? If so, may they exterminate the minority? How much voice may they have in being governed? One can imagine Hitler's claiming that under the above definition, Germany qualifies as a democracy, since Hitler represents ideals by which a majority of Germans freely chose to be governed in electing him their leader. Vagueness can be reduced by providing adequate definitions, using examples, restating your point in a different way, in short, by spelling out in detail what you mean.

Second, avoid ambiguity. Ambiguity occurs when the reader is unsure which among several possible meanings of an expression is intended, although each meaning may be relatively clear by itself. A common fallacy of ambiguity is to begin an essay using a term to mean one thing and then to switch implicitly to another meaning without informing your reader. For example, a student recently wrote an essay in which he sometimes used the term "mind" in a collective sense to mean "the sum-total of one's particular experiences, dispositions, and thoughts," and at other times used it in a substantial sense connoting a thing, "a container or repository of particular thoughts and experiences." Such ambiguous expression greatly reduces clarity.

Third, minimize the use of technical or profound-sounding expressions and, when you do rely on them, clarify them immediately. A few examples of such expressions are 'reality', 'absolute', 'subjective', 'essence', 'inner self', 'cosmic', 'power structure', and 'establishment mentality'. Covering as much territory as they do, their elasticity makes them often unsuitable for precisely formulating and analyzing a problem. Unless you clearly fix their meanings, such expressions are open to a variety of connotations, which will both confuse the reader and allow him to read too much into your view. They lend themselves to vagueness and ambiguity. For these reasons, avoid also such cliches as "Seeing is believing," "It all depends on your point of view," and "Everyone must march to the music he hears." These reveal your unwillingness to think through what you are writing.

Fourth, do not rely heavily on metaphors and analogies. For example, time has been metaphorically likened to a river that passes from out of the future into the past. And the world has been compared to a giant, complex machine. Although using metaphors and analogies is often helpful in presenting philosophical ideas since they may shed light where ordinary language fails, their capacity to enlighten is equalled by their capacity to mislead. The world is not *just* like a machine. Some have argued that without man's interference, nature's balance exhibits an efficient order and continuity unmatched by any machine. Depending on the point you wish to make, considering all the ways in which the world is and is not like a machine might result in your dropping the analogy altogether. Metaphors and analogies should be used in addition to, but never in place of, straightforward argumentation.

Again, make what *you mean* and what your *words mean* harmonize. Choose your words carefully and write exactly what you mean. For example, you may wish to describe a kleptomaniac as one who does not act freely. You may express this by saying that the kleptomaniac steals "automatically." But this expression would not be saying what you want to say, because there is no incompatibility between acting freely and acting automatically. What you probably meant is that the kleptomaniac acts compulsively, though what your words mean is that he acts without deliberation, spontaneously. So it is important to keep in mind that the words you use may mean something that you do not intend to convey. To help avoid this situation, ask yourself "*What* do I want to say?" and "*How* can I say it most effectively?"

Using examples. In Chapter III, we noted how examples help to clarify meaning. Using examples is particularly important in writing your philosophy essay. Appropriate examples will reduce vagueness and help to keep both you and your reader from getting lost in generalities and abstractions.

First, remember that examples are not arguments. As illustrative devices, they do not demonstrate the truth of your case, although they do help to clarify meaning. For instance, citing Jesus, Socrates, and Ghandi may help to illustrate what you *mean* by the expression 'social revolutionary'. But doing so does not prove that these three men were, in fact, social revolutionaries. To prove that, argumentation is required.

Second, it is often helpful to think through the *relation* between the example you cite and what it is supposed to exemplify. This helps to avoid confusion and increase precision. For instance, your essay may revolve around the concept of a supreme being. As particular examples you cite God (Judeo-Christian), Allah, and Brahman. These instances, however, illustrate very different types of supreme beings. In fact, the impersonal Brahman differs so radically from the colorful creator, Allah, that Brahman probably should not be classified as a supreme being at all. So if your discussion refers only to the concept of a creator-God to which we ascribe certain humanlike qualities, citing Brahman would probably confuse your reader, not clarify your case.

Finally, it is important that your examples be *specific* enough to carry the weight of illustration. For instance, if you attempt to show what it would be like to act always according to the golden rule, you must give enough detail so that your reader knows what acting according to such a rule would actually come to. To be more specific, would judges have to release criminals on the grounds that they, the judges, would not want to be sent to prison themselves? Or is this a misapplication of the golden rule? Tying your case down to particular examples will improve clarity.

Writing well. In closing, it may be helpful to mention a few matters regarding your style of writing. Entire books have been devoted to the topics of writing style and grammar.[2] The following are a few practical suggestions regarding style related to achieving clarity.

First, unless you are a relatively polished writer, keep your sentences short. Doing so will help you to express one idea at a time and thereby increase precision. Similarly, avoid wordiness. For example, the poorly executed sentence "What we see out there in the external world is really there" can be rewritten simply as "We see the world as it is" and still express the same point.

Second, use transitional devices such as "Let us now turn to our first argument," and "Following my presentation of theory X I shall offer two criticisms of it." Using devices that tell your reader where you've been and where you expect to go will help keep both of you on track and will guide him naturally through the sections of your paper to the conclusion. Also, in longer essays it is often helpful occasionally to recapitulate in a brief paragraph or two the substance of your argument up to that point.

Third, do not pad your essay with useless additions, such as too many examples for a single point, apologies for not having shown more than you did, restatements of the obvious, and extended quotations. Quotations, in particular, should be included only when there is a reason for giving someone's exact words — for example, when a question of interpretation is at issue. Padding diverts your reader's interest from the important points you wish to make.

Fourth, write in the active voice rather than in the passive voice. Although writing in the passive voice is not necessarily less clear than writing in the active voice, too much passive voice fatigues your reader and is less likely to make a forceful impression on him. For example, instead of writing "Theory X was earlier shown by me to be false," write "I have demonstrated that theory X is false."

Fifth, don't overwork such indefinite terms as 'this', 'that', 'which', 'thing', and 'idea'; be specific. Of course, such terms are sound aids to normal exposition. When overused, however, they frequently generate vagueness and confusion, particularly regarding what they refer to. Suppose in your examination of a philosopher's position you cite two claims that he makes and then state: "I shall now argue that this is false." Here, the antecedent is ambiguous, for it is not clear whether 'this' refers to both claims or to one of them or, if it refers to one of them, which one it refers to. As an alternative, you might say: "I shall now argue that the second claim, 'The end always justifies the means,' is false."

In conclusion, we have surveyed only a few of the points that will help you develop your philosophy essay. Of course, no foolproof method or mechanical procedure for writing philosophy clearly and coherently has been offered, since no such method exists. Philosophical ability, as manifested in clear and cogent thinking and writing, is one of the arts of life — to be cultivated by anyone having the willingness to think and the spirit to endeavor.

Notes

1.   You will probably want to consider other critical questions, too, such
      as: "Do the arguments show something other than what they are
      intended to show?"; "Has the writer properly interpreted the prob-
      lem?"; "Are the central claims mutually consistent?"; "Has the writer
      subtly changed the meaning of key terms?"; and "Is the theory
      sufficiently developed and exemplified?"

2.   A helpful and concise text devoted to elementary rules of style and
      grammar is William Strunk, Jr. and E. B. White, *The Elements of Style*
      (New York: Macmillan, 1959). A widely used text about the mechanics
      of constructing term papers is Kate Turabian, *A Manual for Writers of
      Term Papers, Theses, and Dissertations*, 3rd ed. (University of Chicago
      Press, 1967).

Answers to Selected Exercises

I.   A.   (1)   This is an empirical claim. If it is intended to be applicable to *all* persons, it is most likely false. It is of no philosophical interest.

(2)   This assertion implies a logical exclusion between 'happiness' and 'exclusive self-concern'. It is also probably intended to imply that devoting one's time, thoughts, and so on to other persons is a a necessary condition of being happy. It is of some philosophical interest, particularly for ethics.

(3)   The term 'basis' is ambiguous. It may imply a contingent causal relation such that the desire to be happy is what allegedly makes persons develop moral standards. Or it may imply that any adequate moral standard must judge rightness and wrongness in relation to the happiness generated by an action. The latter sense is of philosophical interest.

(4)   This claim expresses a logical truth. It is true of anything. For example, there are only two types of cars in the world, Chevrolets and non-Chevrolets. It is neither empirically nor philosophically controversial.

(5)   This claim expresses a definition of 'happiness'. Its adequacy largely depends on how

one interprets 'desires'. It is philosophically interesting.

II.   D.   Day regularly precedes (follows) night, yet does not cause the occurrence of night.

F.   Many beliefs held strongly and sincerely nevertheless turn out to be false, for example, that the earth is the center of the universe. To know something, it must be true as well as believed. (Can you think of any other conditions?)

G.   A misstatement would normally be interpreted as unintentional, for example, a slip of the tongue. Lies are intentional. A dozen examples of the difference should come to mind.

III. C.   This argument is valid. It corresponds to the *modus ponens* argument form.

IV.   B.   One questionable assumption is that the exclusive cause of all criminal acts is environmental rather than genetic; that is, there are no "born" criminals.

D.   A questionable assumption is that physical maturity implies intellectual and, in particular, political maturity.

I.   A questionable assumption of this passage is that to truly appreciate and understand something, one must have directly experienced it from the "inside."

V.   B.   Since this statement is itself a generalization, then it must be false also. Hence, it is self-refuting.

F.   Without certain qualifications, this prescription is self-defeating in a practical sense. For example, it may be in someone's self-interest to kill the person who makes the prescription. And this consequence is not in the latter person's interest.

H.   Fast or slow passage of any process takes place with respect to time. For example, it takes Smith two hours to swim a mile, whereas it takes Jones only twenty minutes. Thus, for time itself to pass slowly, we must postulate a second, higher-level, time to measure the passage of the first time. Higher-level times would have to be postulated for each level at which we wished to say that time passed quickly or slowly. Of course, if we identify time with some physical process, for example, movement of a clock's hands, we could avoid these objectionable consequences. "Faster" time would simply be faster motion of the hands. In this case, however, you might then ask yourself, "Faster with respect to what?"

VI.   A.   Many persons have a very strong will to do something, for example, cease heroin addiction, yet are unable to do so. You should resist the temptation to interpret this platitude in a completely nonfalsifiable way that makes it immune to counterexample — that is, of supposing that *whenever* someone tries but fails, he or she didn't really try hard enough.

       C.   This passage expresses an extremely narrow conception of the purpose of dramatic acting. One might just as easily suppose that its purpose is to convey a theme or message or even to bring pleasure to the actors themselves.

       E.   This passage does not express even a partially adequate conception of philosophy, since it rests on the false assumption that the philosopher's concern is basically with the causes of holding certain beliefs. You may recall from earlier discussion that the social pressures that may cause one to be a political conservative, for example, have nothing to do with the rational justification of a conservative political philosophy.

VII.   A.   This argument begs the issue, since one of the premises used to prove that the laws against homosexuality are good already expresses a negative value judgment against homosexuality. To avoid begging the issue, the view that homosexuality is immoral must be supported with further non-question-begging reasons.

F.   This argument is not question-begging. It is, however, invalid.

I.   This argument begs the issue against Russell, since it is part of his hypothesis that objects that now appear to be millions of years old actually came into being at an advanced age.

Suggested Readings

Anthologies

Alston, W. E. and Brandt, R. B. *The Problems of Philosophy*, 2nd ed. Boston: Allyn and Bacon, 1974.

Bierman, A. and Gould, J. *Philosophy for a New Generation*, 2nd ed. New York: Macmillan, 1973.

Bronstein, D. J.; Krikorian, Y. H.; and Wiener, P. P. *Basic Problems of Philosophy*, 4th ed. Englewood Cliffs, N.J.: Prentice-Hall, 1972.

Burr, J. R. and Goldinger, M. *Philosophy and Contemporary Issues*. New York: Macmillan, 1972.

Edwards, P. and Pap, A. *A Modern Introduction to Philosophy*, 3rd ed. New York: The Free Press, 1973.

Feinberg, J. *Reason and Responsibility*, 2nd ed. Encino, Calif.: Dickenson, 1971.

Rachels, J. and Tillman, F. *Philosophical Issues: A Contemporary Introduction*. New York: Harper and Row, 1972.

Struhl, P. R. and Struhl, K. J. *Philosophy Now: An Introductory Reader*. New York: Random House, 1972.

Tillman, F. A.; Berofsky, B.; and O'Connor, J. *Introductory Philosophy*, 2nd ed. New York: Harper and Row, 1971.

Westphal, F. *The Art of Philosophy*. Englewood Cliffs, N.J.: Prentice-Hall, 1972.

Wolff, R. P. *Philosophy: A Modern Encounter*, basic ed. Englewood Cliffs, N.J.: Prentice-Hall, 1973.

Commentaries

Beardsley, E. and Beardsley, M. *Invitation to Philosophical Thinking*. New York: Harcourt Brace Jovanovich, 1972.

Clark, M. *The Need to Question*. Englewood Cliffs, N.J.: Prentice-Hall, 1973.

Cornman, J. and Lehrer, K. *Philosophical Problems and Arguments*, 2nd ed. New York: Macmillan, 1974.

Halverson, W. *A Concise Introduction to Philosophy*. New York: Random House, 1969.

Katen, T. E. *Doing Philosophy*. Englewood Cliffs, N.J.: Prentice-Hall, 1973.

Reid, C. L. *Basic Philosophical Analysis*. Encino, Calif.: Dickenson, 1971.
Stroll, A. and Popkin, R. *Introduction to Philosophy*, 2nd ed. New York: Holt, Reinhart and Winston, 1972.
Westphal, F. *The Activity of Philosophy*. Englewood Cliffs, N.J.: Prentice-Hall, 1969.
Wheatley, J. *Prolegomena to Philosophy*. Belmont, Calif.: Wadsworth, 1970.

Readings on the nature of philosophy

Bronstein, D. J.; Krikorian, Y. H.; and Wiener, P. P. *Basic Problems of Philosophy*, 4th ed. Englewood Cliffs, N.J.: Prentice-Hall, 1972. Chapter One contains classic selections by William James, C. D. Broad, and Bertrand Russell, among others, concerning the subject matter, purposes, and methods of philosophy.
Copi, I. *Introduction to Logic*, 4th ed. New York: Macmillan, 1972. A good elementary survey of the techniques of inductive and deductive reasoning, methods of definition, and informal logical fallacies.
Emmet, E. R. *Learning to Philosophize*. Harmondsworth, England: Penguin, 1968. An elementary exposition of how certain philosophical problems arise and how they may be critically examined.
Gorovitz, S. and Williams, R. G. *Philosophical Analysis: An Introduction to Its Language and Techniques*, 2nd ed. New York: Random House, 1969. A more advanced exposition of the central tools of analytic philosophy.
Hook, S. "Does Philosophy Have a Future?" In *The Range of Philosophy*, edited by H. Titus and Maylon Hepp. New York: Van Nostrand, Reinhold, 1970. A very readable survey of alternative purposes of philosophy.
Johnstone, H., ed. *What Is Philosophy?* New York: Macmillan, 1965. A collection of articles representing a broad spectrum of views about the nature of philosophy.
Kennick, W. and Lazerowitz, M., eds. *Metaphysics: Readings and Reappraisals*. Englewood Cliffs, N.J.: Prentice-Hall, 1967. Included are essays by A. J. Ayer, Brand Blanshard, John Passmore, and Morris Lazerowitz, which, although they are devoted to defending or criticizing various conceptions of metaphysics, are relevant to many areas of philosophy in general.
Lange, J. *The Cognitivity Paradox*. Princeton, N.J.: Princeton University Press, 1970. An advanced yet readable analysis of the concept of a philosophical problem.
Passmore, J. "Philosophy," In *Encyclopedia of Philosophy*, edited by Paul Edwards. New York: Macmillan, 1967. Incorporates a survey of historically significant conceptions of philosophy together with a brief exposition of the author's own views.
Singer, P. "Philosophers Are Back on the Job," *New York Times Magazine*, 7 July, 1974. An interesting discussion of certain views about the purposes and subject matter of philosophy, including a defense of the relevance of philosophical thinking for ethical issues.

White, A. R. *The Philosophy of Mind.* New York: Random House, 1967. Chapter One contains a lucid explanation of the conceptual nature of philosophical problems.

Wilson, J. *Thinking with Concepts.* New York: Cambridge University Press, 1963. An elementary exposition of some characteristics of philosophical problems and a helpful survey of critical tools, from the standpoint of a contemporary analytic philosopher.

Index